# BACKCOUNTRYSKI!
## OREGON

### CLASSIC DESCENTS FOR SKIERS & SNOWBOARDERS, INCLUDING SOUTHWEST WASHINGTON

## CHRISTOPHERVANTILBURG

SASQUATCH BOOKS
SEATTLE

Printed in the United States of America
Distributed in Canada by Raincoast Books, Ltd.
08 07 06 05 04 03 02 01          5 4 3 2 1

Cover, interior design, and composition: Kate Basart
Cover photograph:  Greg Von Doersten
Interior photographs: Christopher Van Tilburg
Mapmaker: Marlene Kocur

Library of Congress Cataloging in Publication Data
Van Tilburg, Christopher
    Backcountry ski! Oregon : classic descents for skiers & snowboarders, including southwest
    Washington / Christopher Van Tilburg.
          p.          cm.
    ISBN 1-57061-232-3 (alk. paper)
    1. Cross-country skiing—Oregon—Guidebooks. 2. Cross-country skiing—Washington
    (State)—Guidebooks. 3. Cross-country ski trails—Oregon—Guidebooks. 4. Cross-country
    ski trails—Washington (State)—Guidebooks. 5. Snowboarding—Oregon—Guidebooks. 6.
    Snowboarding—Washington (State)—Guidebooks. 7. Oregon—Guidebooks. 8. Washington
    (State)—Guidebooks. I. Title
    GV854.5.O7 V36 2001
    796.93'2'09795—dc21                                                    00-049662

IMPORTANT NOTE: Please use common sense. No guidebook can act as a substitute for
careful planning and appropriate training. Know your personal limits; it is incumbent upon any
user of this guide to assess his or her own skills, experience, fitness, and equipment. There is
inherent danger in skiing and snowboarding and in the routes described in this book, and read-
ers must assume responsibility for their own actions and safety. Changing or unfavorable conditions in weather, roads, trails, waterways, etc. cannot be anticipated by the author or publisher,
but should be considered by any outdoor participants, as trails may become dangerous or slopes
unrideable due to such altered conditions. Likewise, be aware of any changes in public jurisdic-
tion. Do not ski on private property without permission. The author and the publisher will not
be responsible or liable for your safety or the consequences of using this guide.
    The information in this edition is based on facts available at press time and is subject to
change. The author and publisher welcome information or updates conveyed by users of this
book.

SASQUATCH BOOKS
615 Second Avenue
Seattle, Washington 98104
(206) 467-4300
books@SasquatchBooks.com
www.SasquatchBooks.com

*For Avrie*

# OREGON & SOUTHWEST WASHINGTON

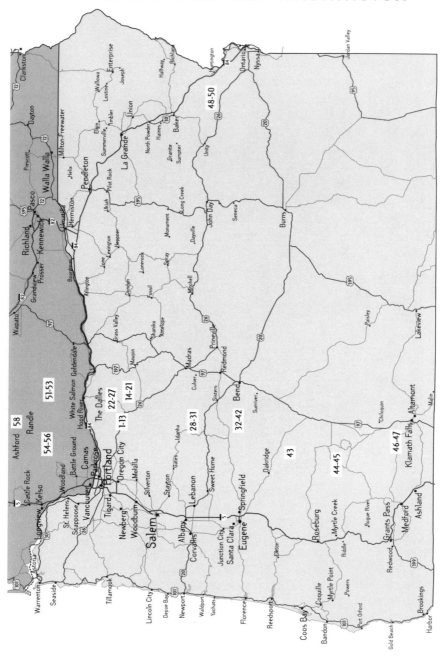

# Contents

# Acknowledgments

I owe many thanks for assistance to friends, family, and colleagues. Geoff Richardson rode many of the routes with me and took some of the photos. Several people helped with route development and review, especially Roger Averbeck at Wing Ridge Ski Tours and numerous U. S. Forest Service rangers and staff. Thanks to the Mazamas for use of their excellent library, including their trip prospectuses and back issues of their journal.

Thanks to several equipment suppliers, including CamelBak, DaKine, Duotone, GoLite, Leki, Life Link, Patagonia, Suunto, Tubbs Snowshoes, and Voile.

The crew at Sasquatch Books has been wonderful to work with, especially editor Kate Rogers, project editor Laura Gronewold, and designer Kate Basart, as well as mapmaker Marlene Kocur, copy editor Heath Lynn Silberfeld, and proofreader Sigrid Asmus.

My parents, Wayne and Eleanor, taught me how to ski. My wife, Jennifer Wilson, taught me more about mountains than anyone. My girls, Skylar and Avrie, rode along for scouting missions. All my colleagues in the Pacific Northwest's many ski patrols, mountain rescue units, mountaineering and ski clubs, and Forest Service districts, as well as the National Park Service, continue to help make Oregon's and Washington's mountains accessible and safe.

# Preface

I was three years old when I first skied down the field in our backyard in rural Southwest Washington. I put my feet atop Dad's 205-cm red skis and we careened down the cow pasture to the barn. We hiked back up and did it again and again. I was soaked by the heavy wet snow affectionately known as "Pacific Northwest crud" or "Cascade cement." Later, Mom had a cup of hot chocolate waiting inside for me by a warm fire.

A few years later my parents bought me short red skis and matching boots. We walked up the slope at Summit Ski Area on Mount Hood and glided back down. At first I went down while held in my parents' arms between their legs. Later I began going down by myself, straight down. The next year I graduated to the T-bar. On my first ride up it nearly knocked me over. The bar came across my shoulder blades and hit Dad across his knees, and he had to hunch over to keep me from falling off.

From grade school through college, I skied resorts on Mount Hood and elsewhere. I went away to Europe and Utah. When I returned, I was spending more time in the backcountry than in-area, I was snowboarding, and I was doing both year-round. I climbed and snowboarded Mounts Hood, Adams, and St. Helens. Like all mountaineers, I began researching new routes, particularly snowboard descents in Oregon's Cascades. I decided to put together a collection of routes for skiers and snowboarders, for all levels and all seasons. I started keeping a log of my descents, and then this book came about.

While researching and writing this book, I took time to step back. My wife and I bought my two-year-old daughter a pair of 80-cm skis and size 7 boots. On Mount Hood we began to teach her the beauty of snow and mountains, first between our legs and then on her own. So the cycle continues in these mountains. Many happy turns!

# About These Mountains

There's one thing unique about skiing and snowboarding the Oregon and Southwest Washington Cascades: We make turns year-round. We may not always have deep, dry powder or endless days of clear, cold weather, but we can snowboard and ski every month of the year pretty much without fail. We have our share of powder in winter, smooth corn in spring, and reliable firn in summer. A light snowfall gives us a bonus in fall.

The South Cascades are an assorted lot. Most routes here are on the snow-capped stratovolcanos, which are either dormant, extinct, or active. For example, Mount Hood vents sulfur gas from fumaroles near the summit and Mount St. Helens steams from its crater. In winter trails are snow-covered, but by spring or summer the approaches are marked by the ubiquitous basalt and andesite lava. Glaciers and permanent snowfields are found on many peaks and provide media for many of our turns.

The routes in this book are for skiers and snowboarders. There is some discussion regarding what we should call this type of backcountry travel or mountaineering. The basic activity includes climbing the slope, then gliding down with an edged snow tool. Several terms have been suggested, such as "glisse alpinism" (glisse derived from the French *glisser*, to glide, and brought into popular use by Colorado writer Louis Dawson), "snow gliding or riding," "ski and snowboard mountaineering," and "backcountry skiing and snowboarding." The whole idea of separate sports gets more confusing with splitboarding, where the snowboard splits into two skis for ascent; a rider skis up and snowboards down. Moreover, with skiing you have a number of styles, all requiring different equipment and technique, such as alpine, telemark, alpine touring, cross-country, and firn gliding, as discussed later in this chapter.

Whatever you call it, these routes have been assembled for both skiers and snowboarders. Most of the time you will be doing one or the other, but you may be using a splitboard or going with mixed groups of skiers and snowboarders. Some routes are better for snowboards, usually because of snow conditions. Some are better for skiers, usually because of terrain. Though I have occasionally noted this information in the route descriptions, conditions are widely variable from season to season and year to year.

These routes have been selected with a few basic concepts in mind, besides the fact that they are great thrills for all glisse alpinists. First, they provide something for everyone from beginners looking to make their first backcountry turns in Oregon to ski and snowboard mountaineers wanting to ride from the summits. Keep in mind that a beginner backcountry skier or snowboarder is equal to an advanced intermediate or an expert in developed resort areas.

Second, these routes provide a good selection for year-round riding: Some are primarily spring and summer routes, while others are only snow-covered in winter. Many can be ridden throughout the year, depending on conditions.

Third, most of these routes are aesthetically rewarding tours: thrilling, beautiful, or otherwise well worth the trip. Technical routes beyond basic glacier travel and those descents not worth hours of slogging to and fro have been omitted.

I have included some routes in developed ski areas. My brother gave me an interesting book while I was researching this one, *Northwest Ski Trails*, published in 1968, which contains descriptions of both ski resorts and backcountry routes. As interest in backcountry skiing and snowboarding surged in the 1990s, guidebooks proliferated but included strictly out-of-area routes. However, many backcountry skiers and snowboarders start out by hiking and descending ski-area slopes before, during, or after the season. Likewise, many resorts nowadays have open-boundary policies that allow one to ride a lift up, then hike out of bounds. Since this is an integral part of today's backcountry, I include some routes in and around ski resorts.

A word of caution: If you plan to ride a lift and then hike out of bounds, you should travel with permission from the ski patrol of that area. This is both your legal and ethical duty. Call ahead and check in with the patrol before you start out in a ski area. Not all resorts allow lift access for out-of-bounds skiing or snowboarding.

I have been on the mountains at all times of year, in varied conditions, and in all forms of ascent and descent: on alpine skis, cross-country skis, snowboard, splitboard, snowshoes, crampons, bike, boots, and, where roads and laws allow, a truck. Some I have climbed recently, others a while ago. I have researched them at different times of the year, in different conditions. By excluding seasonal landmarks, I have kept the route descriptions useful without limiting them to specific times. I also have not made these routes so detailed as to take out the adventure. I have corroborated my firsthand information with others' descriptions of the routes, as well as with numerous maps and through conversations with Forest Service rangers, ski patrollers, mountain rescue personnel, and Pacific Northwest ski and snowboard mountaineers.

You should supplement this book with conversations with rangers, topographic maps, other guidebooks, and the like. You should know how to find your way with a map, compass, and altimeter. Although this book should travel with you in your vehicle, you shouldn't plan to carry it in your pack.

If you are new to the backcountry, consider hiring one of the many guide services. In fact, several routes in this book, including Mount Hood, Mount Bailey, and the Wallowas, feature guided backcountry tours. Think about taking a guided trip as an introduction to these volcanos. You will learn new skills, make friends, and get to know an area with a seasoned guide. Also, consider taking a local avalanche-training course from one of the guide services.

## Equipment

This book is designed for all snow gliders. Skiers may use one of several types of ski and binding systems. Alpine touring (also known as ski mountaineering or randonee) gear is great for a wide variety of conditions and terrain. The free heel allows ascent with skis and skins and the bindings lock down for the descent. Many prefer telemark gear. Compared to alpine touring, these bindings connect only your boot toe to the ski, allowing a free heel for ascent and descent. Many of these routes are suitable for Nordic touring gear (steel-edged cross-country skis with or without scales on the bases). Those few who are just starting out or occasionally venturing into the backcountry may even use their downhill ski gear with ski-mountaineering adapters in the bindings. These adapters fit between the alpine ski boot and binding to allow for hiking up with a free-heel mechanism. They are removed and stored in a pack for descent. The mountaineer who wants to take along skis for the occasional summer descent might choose firn gliders or figles, small 100-cm skis you can throw on your pack for the hike up and then use to glide down on the summer corn.

It is mandatory that snowboarders have a method for ascent. Many riders use snowshoes because they are readily available and relatively inexpensive. Short skis are becoming more popular, especially for snowboarders who tour with skiers or want to use a skin track.

More and more riders are using splitboards, also called "touring boards." A seam running lengthwise allows the board to be split into two halves. The bindings are removed, the board split into two skis, and the bindings reattached in ski fashion. This allows riders to ski up with climbing skins and reassemble the snowboard for the ride down.

In the case of steep routes, crampons may be required as well, depending on conditions. Instep or ski/splitboard crampons may be used in lieu of full-frame front pointers in some cases.

In addition to ski and snowboard gear, you should carry—and know how to use—backcountry gear for every one of these routes. This includes essentials such as food, water, map, compass, altimeter, fire starter, first-aid kit, extra clothes, sunscreen, sunglasses, repair kit, headlamp, and an emergency shelter. Mandatory avalanche gear includes a transceiver (also called a "beacon"), shovel, and probe. You must practice regularly and learn to use this equipment before you attempt these routes. Formal instruction is especially important for avalanche rescue, navigation, and survival. Consult avalanche and mountain safety texts and take a course in avalanche safety and general mountaineering.

A few routes require more advanced equipment, such as basic alpine gear: a helmet, crampons, ice ax, wands, rope, harness, snow anchors, and crevasse rescue gear. You must be well-versed in glacier travel and crevasse rescue techniques before undertaking these routes.

## Weather and Snow

Oregon and Southwest Washington's weather can be predictable, as storms typically come in with advance notice. Occasionally, local weather systems or rapidly advancing storms arrive unexpectedly.

To find good snow, watch the weather all year long, in addition to checking the weather forecast before you go. Learn the snow and weather patterns and keep a close eye on seasonal and weekly variations. Watch the snowfall, temperature, and wind. Learn the effects of prolonged sun or rain on the snowpack. Meteorology is a complex science, and I highlight only a few key points below.

The most complete source for Oregon and Southwest Washington skiers and snowboarders is the Northwest Weather and Avalanche Center at 503/808-2400 or www.nwac.noaa.gov. Another great source is the National Weather Service at 503/261-9246 in Portland, 360/694-6136 in Southwest Washington, or www.nws.noaa.gov in cyberspace.

In Oregon and Washington, storms usually come from the Pacific Ocean. Southwest storms that come from the tropics are warm and wet, the so-called "Pineapple Express." These bring heavy, wet, gooey snow—and sometimes rain—to the South Cascades. Storms from west-southwest or west-northwest are cooler and drier but still contain a lot of moisture and often dump snow in the Oregon mountains. The storms from the north are usually cold and bring less moisture, although the snow that falls is typically light and dry.

Follow the freezing and snow levels (the snow level is usually 1,000 feet below the freezing level). Dry and plentiful snow is generally found 1,000 to 2,000 feet above the freezing level, which corresponds to 2,000 to 3,000 feet above the snow level. The air temperature there is probably about 20° to 25°F. The east side of the Cascades has less snow, but the weather is clearer and the snow is drier. The west flanks generally get more snow, but it is significantly heavier and wetter.

In spring and summer, timing is everything: Go early in the day. Many routes must be climbed in the early morning hours when the snow is firm. The best descents are done midmorning, when the snow softens to corn but before it turns to slush. In winter, start early since daylight hours are limited.

Aspect is another important function of snow conditions. East- and south-facing slopes heat up and get warm and slushy quickly during spring and summer afternoons. North-facing slopes often have good snow, even days after a winter storm.

In addition to snow and weather, the yearly and seasonal variations can be dramatic. Some approach trails may be covered by snow in winter, which makes a longer approach but often allows you to ski or snowboard all the way back to your vehicle. In summer, lava or dirt can significantly speed your approach time, but you will be hiking, not riding, back to your vehicle. Always call ahead to check road and trail conditions.

## Roads

Many roads can be quite hazardous in Oregon and Southwest Washington, not just those in the mountains. Ice, snow, and freezing rain make roads especially treacherous. Always check conditions before driving, carry emergency supplies in your vehicle, and abide by traction requirements. In Oregon, call 800/977-6368 or check www.odot.state.or.us/roads for the road report. In Washington, check 888/766-4636 or www.wsdot.wa.gov/sno-info.

In Oregon, the "Snow Zone" signs are important to follow for safety. They can be almost as confusing as permits, especially with the new tires for "severe snow conditions" now being used in place of studded snow tires. Oregon Department of Transportation (ODOT) defines a traction tire as a studded tire or a tire that qualifies for use in severe snow conditions and is so designated by the snowflake-in-a-mountain logo on the sidewall.

"Carry Chains or Traction Tires" means you must have tire chains in your car that you can put on if you need them or your vehicle must be equipped with traction tires.

"Chains Required: Traction Tires Allowed on Vehicles under 10,000 GVW" means you must have chains on or be using traction tires (either studs or the severe snow condition tires). Four-wheel- or all-wheel-drive units are exempt if they meet the following criteria: weigh less than 6,500 pounds; use traction, mud and snow, or all-weather tires on all four wheels; carry chains; are not towing; and are driven safely.

In Washington, the guidelines are different. "Approved Traction Tires Advised" and "Approved Traction Tires Required" means it is either recommended or mandated that you use qualifying traction tires. Traction tires are defined as studded tires, or those that are designated all-season, all-weather, or mud and snow; they must have the M+S on the sidewall.

"Chains Required" means you must be using chains on the drive tires. Studded tires are not exempt. Four-wheel-drive units are exempt as long as drivers meet certain requirements: engage the four-wheel-drive, use approved traction tires on all four wheels, and carry a set of chains.

## Mountain Safety

Mountain hazards are myriad, including avalanche dangers. Go with a guide, take a course, go with experienced people, study books, and always use caution and good judgment. I do little more here than list the hazards. Mountain weather and route-finding failures are what cause most people trouble: The weather turns bad and they lose their way. Always carry and know how to use your maps, compass, and altimeter. Stay on route and avoid foul weather. Be skilled at building an emergency snow trench or cave and carry gear for an unexpected night out.

Avalanche safety is paramount for skiers and snowboarders. Learn the general guidelines for safety and obtain the general recommendations for that day from the Northwest Weather and Avalanche Center at 503/808-2400 or www.nwac.noaa.gov. Keep in mind that the avalanche report is only general and does not offer specifics. Also remember that an avalanche beacon, shovel, and probe will only help you save your buried buddy; they won't keep you from getting caught. Avoiding avalanches in the first place is the primary safety method.

Weather can pose additional environmental problems. Cold weather can lead to hypothermia and frostbite. The sun and heat can lead to dehydration, sunburn, and snow blindness. Hazards such as lightning, rock fall, ice fall, tree wells, deep snow, high altitude, and crevasses are daily concerns on these routes. Always give yourself a margin for safety. If the snow, weather, or terrain conditions are questionable, stay in-area or find another activity off the mountain.

This book is a guide to mountain wilderness in Oregon and Southwest Washington, and it assumes the reader will be well-versed both in backcountry mountain travel at all times of year, including winter, and skilled in skiing or snowboarding. This is *not* a cross-country skiing book. Beginner routes in this volume will correspond with an advanced or expert route in a comparable cross-country or snowshoe guide. A reasonable measure of ability is being able to safely make turns on the most difficult in-area ski run, in the most difficult weather and snow conditions. In other words, if you can ski or snowboard a black-diamond run, on ice, in a whiteout, and you have experience in mountain wilderness, you are probably ready for the backcountry.

Keep in mind that this guidebook is not an instruction book. Backcountry skiing and snowboarding are advanced technical sports requiring formal instruction, lot of practice, and years of experience. If you are just starting out, take a guided trip or course from a local outfitter or club.

A final note: Oregon has a law that levies a fine against irresponsible and/or unprepared persons requiring rescue, including backcountry skiers and snowboarders. There is no such specific law in Washington.

# Using This Guide

This book is divided into five sections. Each general area is then divided into chapters that describe a specific area.

## Chapter Overviews

Each chapter begins with a general overview of the area and important resources such as information centers, snow reports, and maps. The chapter openings offer a handy reference to important information for planning a tour. Following are brief descriptions of what is provided.

### Maps

The maps named cover an entire area and provide a good lay of the land, especially roads and large drainages. The U.S. Forest Service publishes forest, ranger district, and wilderness area maps that cover large areas. Geo-Graphics wilderness maps provide excellent detail of most Oregon wilderness areas and show topography as well. Green Trails maps show large areas and include summer and winter trails and topography, but they are not as detailed as others. Most of these maps are available at outdoor stores or forest headquarters.

### Primary Info Centers/Ranger Districts

The phone number and web site for the forest headquarters are provided. Some areas may include a recreation report or climber's recording. The local ranger district has the most up-to-date local conditions. Always call ahead to check route conditions and road access. The rangers usually know snow and weather conditions as well. If you can talk to a backcountry ranger, that's a bonus.

### Avalanche/Weather/Road Conditions

The best source is the Northwest Weather and Avalanche Center accessed by phone or via its web site. The National Weather Service also provides updates with links to mountain telemetry data for temperature, precipitation, and wind speed in some areas. Always call ahead to find out what the road conditions are like, especially on mountain passes. Be prepared to follow the state guidelines for traction devices or tires, both for your safety and so you don't get turned back by officials.

## Ski Area Snow Reports

For backcountry routes near ski areas, resort snow phone and web site reports are other ways to get snow and weather conditions.

## Permits

Nowadays, you need a permit for everything and the permit situation for any particular area may change from year to year. You may hear a lot of squabbling in the parking lot about permits and their fees. Keep in mind that permits limit overuse of the land and pay for upkeep of trails, parking areas, and toilets.

For good or ill, one of three types of permits is required on these routes. Because permit requirements vary widely in different areas, each chapter includes an overview of rules and regulations and permits required. Make sure you check well in advance to confirm the requirements listed in this book. In some places, such as Mount Rainier National Park, Mount St. Helens National Volcanic Monument, and Mount Adams, special permits are required.

A wilderness permit is required for all wilderness areas. Such permits are usually available at self-serve boxes at trailheads and are often free, with a few exceptions such as Mount Adams. In addition to the wilderness permit, some areas require a climber's registration form for ascent above timberline to assist with rescues and resource management, so fill it out accurately. Remember to sign out on your way home, if so required.

A sno-park permit is required in winter and spring at most trailheads to help defray costs of plowing. These are available at outdoor stores, ranger stations, and ski areas. In Oregon, a $20 permit lasts from November 15 to April 30. Oregon sno-parks will honor a Washington sno-park pass on a vehicle with Washington license plates. Similarly, Washington will honor Oregon sno-park passes with Oregon plates.

A Northwest Forest Pass is now required year-round on many routes as part of the new recreation fee program. The pass is good for hiking and parking at trailheads in all Oregon and Washington national forests. Cost is $30 a year or $5 a day. These are available at outdoor stores, ranger stations, and self-serve Iron Ranger dispensaries at selected trailheads. In parking areas where a trail park and sno-park pass are both required, usually the sno-park will suffice from November 15 to April 30.

## Of Special Note

Occasionally an area may have particular characteristics that are important to consider for safety and planning.

# Route Descriptions

Each route description begins with essential information. This gives you, at a glance, some information to help plan your trip and compare routes.

## Rip Factor

Denoted at the top of each route by snowflake icons; rip factor is a general guide to the quality of the route. These routes are **highly variable**, especially with regard to snow conditions, weather, yearly changes, and the like. All things considered, this is my **subjective rating on quality**, taking into account steepness, chance of decent snow, views, challenge, approach time, avalanche safety, and other matters. Five snowflakes are generally reserved for the best route or two of the chapter, my favorites. A four-snowflake route is also a must-do. Three snowflakes are reserved for routes that are more technical or those that may have less chance of good snow but still give many thrills. Two snowflakes are for low-angle or low-elevation routes; these are beginner routes near ski areas. One snowflake is saved for routes that have difficult approaches, technical climbing, or variable conditions; these are probably best saved for last.

## Starting point

This is the elevation at the parking lot and trailhead. Your starting point may be different if you use a ski lift to access the backcountry.

## High point

This is the summit or the goal for the ascent. Your elevation may change should you choose a variation or turn around early.

## Drive distance/time

This is the approximate one-way mileage and hours of driving from Portland to the trailhead. Distance and times from Bend, Salem, Eugene, or other towns will be different. Plan much more time if the road and weather conditions are poor. Drive safely!

## Trail distance/time

This is the approximate round-trip mileage and hours of travel from the parking area to the high point and back. It is a very rough estimate and doesn't include time for prolonged rest stops or to hike back up to make another run. Your time will depend on what shape you are in, weather, snow, trail conditions, seasonal variances, what you had for breakfast, how well you slept the night before, your group, and many other factors.

In general, time estimates are based on experience and three basic rates. For steep terrain, time is based on one hour per 1,000 feet of elevation gain. For approach trails, the time is based on about two to four miles per hour on dirt trail and one to two miles per hour on snow.

## Skill level

Skill level is variable and quite subjective. For simplicity and to account for differences among riders, I've consolidated ascent and descent difficulty, avalanche hazard, and general mountain hazards into three very general categories.

Beginner routes are most often safe, close to roads and civilization, and have low-angle slopes. For riders with some skill in backcountry winter travel, these routes are good places to start. Remember, beginners in the backcountry should be advanced intermediates or experts in ski resorts and able to safely descend a black-diamond run in any condition (including ice) in any weather (including a whiteout)!

Intermediate routes are for those with some additional skill and experience who want to try more challenging routes. They usually have a moderate slope angle and may require some route finding and avalanche risk assessment. They may involve a long day, a summit of a major volcano, or an overnight.

Advanced routes are for backcountry riders with significant experience under their belts, especially in avalanche safety, survival, and navigation. They are generally longer, steeper, and higher in elevation. Snow and terrain conditions may be variable. They often include ascent and descent of a peak, glacier travel, and an overnight.

## Best season

This is my favorite time to ride these particular routes. Although many of these can be done year-round, certain seasons make some tours magical. Remember, call ahead to check conditions such as snow, terrain, weather, road access, and water runoff, which can vary widely from season to season and year to year.

## Maps

Those listed are the topographic maps that are essential for backcountry travel and route finding. United States Geologic Survey (USGS) 1:24,000 (7.5-minute) maps are available at most outdoor stores or forest headquarters. You can order directly through USGS Information Services, P.O. Box 25286, Denver, CO 80225, 800/USA-MAPS, or mapping.usgs.gov/esic/esic_index.html.

Geo-Graphics has excellent topographic maps for many of the wilderness areas in Oregon and Washington. Similar to USGS maps, Geo-Graphics maps are 1:27,000 scale but are large so they cover an entire wilderness area. They are available at most outdoor stores in Oregon and Washington or through ranger districts. Imus Geographics has topographic wilderness maps for a few areas.

## Getting There

Directions from Portland provide a constant for comparing routes. Routes from Bend, Salem, Eugene, or other towns will be different. Always call ahead and check road conditions and access.

## The Route

The route descriptions are general enough to prevent this book from becoming outdated. Some route details are left for you to discover. Keep in mind that seasonal and yearly variations cause changes in terrain, snowpack, water, and weather, especially for trails, snowfields, landmarks, and vegetation, which may be quite different after a few years. Confirm the route with a ranger or others knowledgeable about area conditions. Use a map to correlate with this book's description.

## Route Maps

Each route description is accompanied by a map showing the general topography, main elevation points, major landmarks, starting and turn-around points, and both the main and alternate routes. Keep in mind that these maps are primarily illustrative; they are not a replacement for the USFS, USGS, Geo-Graphics, or Green Trails maps recommended for each route.

## Map Legend

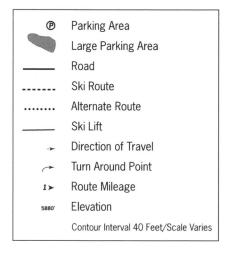

| | |
|---|---|
| ℗ | Parking Area |
| | Large Parking Area |
| —— | Road |
| ------ | Ski Route |
| ........ | Alternate Route |
| —— | Ski Lift |
| ⇀ | Direction of Travel |
| ⤳ | Turn Around Point |
| 1▸ | Route Mileage |
| 5880' | Elevation |
| | Contour Interval 40 Feet/Scale Varies |

# MOUNT HOOD

T

# Mount Hood South

The American Indians called it Wy'east, "Son of the Great Spirit." In 1792, British Lieutenant William Broughton spied it from the Columbia River and named it after Rear Admiral Samuel Hood of the British navy. Today it is known as Mount Hood, almost synonymous with Oregon mountaineering. Although it is a dormant volcano, fumaroles near the summit spew sulfur-scented steam. At 11,239 feet it is one of the most-climbed mountains in the Pacific Northwest and the world. With numbers often compared to Mount Fuji in Japan, Mount Hood has some 10,000 climbers attempting it every year.

The first ascent was by Portland climbers William Buckley, W. Chittenden, James Deardorf, Henry Pittock, and L. Powell in 1857, although *Oregonian* editor Thomas Dryer reportedly reached the summit in 1854. In 1894, the Portland climbing club, the Mazamas, was formed on the summit. Still active today, the club offers ski and snowboard mountaineering courses for members. The first ski descent from the summit was probably accomplished by Sylvain Saudan in 1971.

The south side offers year-round skiing and snowboarding. Timberline Lodge is the launching pad for ski and snowboard mountaineering in Oregon, especially during spring and summer. Mount Hood's south side gives access to a huge variety of routes: beginner backcountry tours, lift-access backcountry trips, ski and snowboard mountaineering routes, and technical pitches. All are doable within a day's adventure. Since road access goes to Timberline Ski Area at 6,500 feet and a ski lift drops one off at 8,500 feet, access to snow at higher elevations is relatively easy.

## Mount Hood South Maps

USFS Mount Hood Wilderness, Geo-Graphics Mount Hood Wilderness, Green Trails Mount Hood 462

## Primary Info Centers/Ranger Districts

Mount Hood National Forest Headquarters, Portland, OR: 503/668-1700, www.fs.fed.us/r6/mthood

Information Center, Welches, OR: 503/622-7674

Zigzag Ranger District: 503/622-3191

## Avalanche/Weather/Road Conditions

Northwest Weather and Avalanche Center: 503/808-2400,
www.nwac.noaa.gov

National Weather Service: 503/261-9246 or 360/694-6136,
www.nws.noaa.gov

Oregon DOT Pass Report: 800/977-6368, www.odot.state.or.us/roads

## Ski Area Snow Reports

Timberline: 503/222-2211, www.timberlinelodge.com

Mount Hood Meadows: 503/227-7669, www.skihood.com

Ski Bowl: 503/222-2695, www.skibowl.com

Summit: 503/272-0256, www.summitskiarea.com

## Permits

A wilderness permit and a climber's registration are required for all routes in
the Mount Hood Wilderness. This begins above Timberline Ski Area on the
south side at around 9,000 feet. Free, self-issued permits and climber's regis-
trations are available at Timberline Ski Area's Wy'east Day Lodge.

A sno-park pass is required for parking between November 15 and April 30.

# Of Special Note

On south-side routes that climb above 9,000 feet, be aware of the "Mount Hood Triangle." If you follow the fall line down from high on the south side, you will descend Zigzag Glacier and the Mississippi Head Cliffs. The correct route down is a slight traverse to the left that generally follows magnetic south on your compass. In a storm or whiteout, it may seem odd not to descend the fall line, but trust your compass!

Mount Hood Locators are available for a nominal charge for south-side mountaineers. The Mount Hood Locator is an animal tracker that was made available for use on the south side after an accident took the lives of nine schoolchildren and adult leaders. It is activated by pulling a pin. If a search-and-rescue team is actively looking for a lost climber, a receiver is used to home in on the transmitter to aid in locating the lost person. It is not designed for immediate rescue and it is *not* an avalanche beacon. Rescuers only use it to find someone reported missing. You may choose to carry one per party, especially if you are attempting the summit. You can rent locators in Government Camp at the Mount Hood Inn, 503/272-3205, and at most mountaineering shops in Portland.

Since some of these routes are partially or entirely within the Timberline Ski Area, they are best ridden before the resort is open for the season, after it closes, or just outside the ski area boundary. Check with the ski patrol for current regulations. Lift-access riding at the time of this writing is allowed above Palmer lift. If you hike during the ski season, hike on the edge of the resort and watch for downhill skiers and snowboarders.

For guides, check with the Mazamas at www.mazamas.org or 503/227-2345.

# MOUNT HOOD SOUTH
# Tom, Dick, and Harry Mountain
❄❄❄

| | |
|---|---|
| Starting point | Mirror Lake trailhead, 3,400 feet |
| High point | Tom, Dick, and Harry Mountain, 5,000 feet |
| Drive distance/time | 60 miles, 1 hour |
| Trail distance/time | 5 miles, 3 hours |
| Skill level | Intermediate |
| Best season | Winter |
| Maps | USGS Government Camp, Geo-Graphics Mount Hood Wilderness |

Tom, Dick, and Harry Mountain is about the closest terrain to Portland for descent turns. When compared to other south-side routes, it's fairly steep. Only a short hike from the road, it is ideal for a half-day tour. However, because it is low in elevation, the snow quality is often lousy. When it finally does dump, the steep shots here are avalanche prone. Nonetheless, if you are a weather-savvy, avalanche-aware, off-piste enthusiast with only a half day to spare, you can get great turns here. On sunny weekends, this basin may be crowded with snowshoers and cross-country skiers.

Ski Bowl with Tom, Dick, and Harry Mountain to right

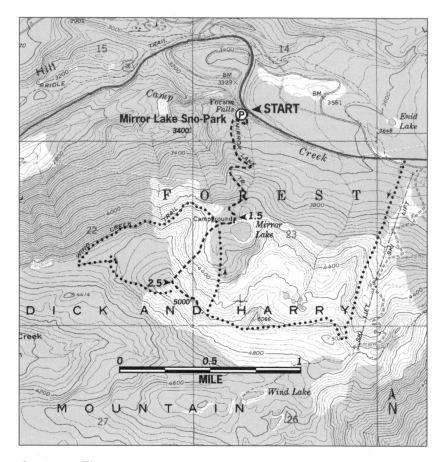

## Getting There

Drive east on U.S. 26 from Portland 60 miles toward Government Camp. About a mile before Government Camp, park at the Mirror Lake Sno-park on the south side of the road. Use caution when entering and exiting. The highway is busy and the parking area is small. With snow on the road, turning in can be treacherous. For the alternative route from Ski Bowl described below, continue another mile and park at the Ski Bowl Ski Area.

## The Route

Follow Mirror Lake Trail 664 for 1.5 miles to the wide clearing at Mirror Lake. This trail is fairly narrow and may have skin or snowshoe tracks. At Mirror Lake, you will have a good view of the bowl and the many options for descent. Skirt the lake to the right, pass through a thick grove of trees, and climb 800 feet to the ridge. Stay to the right near trees as much as possible and evaluate avalanche hazard on the way up.

Alternatively, continue on Trail 664 as it becomes the Wind Creek Trail for 1.5 miles and heads west, then back east, to gently climb the ridge. This route is longer and doesn't allow you to check out slope conditions on the way up.

Yet another option is to hike alongside the Ski Bowl lifts to the top of the ski area and traverse west to Tom, Dick, and Harry Ridge and the bowl that opens up below. Because you will be skiing or snowboarding within the area boundaries, this approach is best reserved for before or after the Ski Bowl season. Check with the ski patrol about access if you want to make this approach during the ski season.

From the ridge you have several options. The west end of Tom, Dick, and Harry offers 25-degree slopes. Toward the east end of the ridge the slopes steepen and you will find some chutes among the rock bands. Use caution, however: With good snow the avalanche hazard is significant.

Ride the slope down to Mirror Lake. You may then need to skin or snowshoe back across the flats. Cruise back down the Mirror Lake Trail. Because of some flat spots on the trail, snowboarders may want to use poles. Watch for others climbing up the trail, which gets crowded. Trees, switchbacks, and blowdown on the trail can make this glide fairly harry at high speeds. If you left your car at Ski Bowl, it is a short hike on the road to your car.

## MOUNT HOOD SOUTH
# 2 Glade Trail

❄❄

| | |
|---|---|
| Starting point | Government Camp, 4,000 feet |
| High point | Timberline Lodge, 5,880 feet |
| Drive distance/time | 60 miles, 1 hour |
| Trail distance/time | 8 miles, 4 hours |
| Skill level | Beginner |
| Best season | Winter |
| Maps | USGS Mount Hood South, Geo-Graphics Mount Hood Wilderness |

The Glade Trail is an old ski trail that connects Timberline Ski Area with Government Camp. It is most often ridden one way from Timberline, but it is an easy up-and-back for beginners, especially for your first tour. The Glade Trail is the most gentle route in this book, so choose a day with fresh, dry snow or firm, cold corn to make this trip worthwhile. With the low elevation, slush is common on this trail; it can be a slow-motion trip down. For the same reason, it is a pretty safe bet when avalanche danger exists on steeper slopes higher up.

## Getting There
Drive east on U.S. 26 from Portland 60 miles to Government Camp. Take the first Government Camp exit and continue east through town. The Glade Trail begins down a dead-end road first marked as "Meldrum Street" and then as "Blossom Lane." No parking is available at the trailhead, so park in a designated sno-park lot in town and walk down the road. The trailhead is at the dead end of Blossom Lane and is marked by a sign.

Alternatively, a one-way trip starts from Timberline Lodge. The well-marked Timberline Road is a few hundred yards east of Government Camp on

Glade trailhead
on Mount Hood

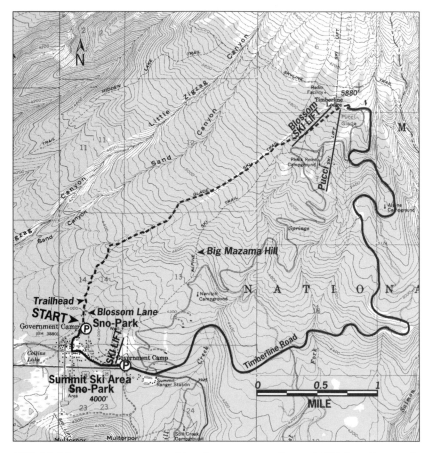

U.S. 26. Most one-way snow riders leave a car at Summit Ski Area Sno-park in Government Camp and get a ride to the top.

## The Route

From Government Camp, follow the well-marked trail through the woods. It meanders through the trees, then opens up to an old powerline swath. After about 4 miles it comes near the bottom of Blossom lift. Continue up to Timberline Lodge, then turn around and glide down.

From Timberline, make turns toward Blossom Lift down the resort slope marked "Glade." About 100 yards before the bottom of Blossom, look for the sign and the wide-open powerline clearing of the Glade Trail. The start is on the north side, or skier's right, of the run and chairlift. Follow the marked signs through the woods to Government Camp.

## MOUNT HOOD SOUTH

# 3 | Alpine Trail

❄ ❄

| | |
|---|---|
| Starting point | Government Camp, 4,000 feet |
| High point | Timberline Lodge, 5,880 feet |
| Drive distance/time | 60 miles, 1 hour |
| Trail distance/time | 5 miles, 3 hours |
| Skill level | Beginner |
| Best season | Winter |
| Maps | USGS Mount Hood South, Geo-Graphics Mount Hood Wilderness |

The Alpine Trail is another old ski trail that connects Timberline Ski Area with Government Camp. It is shorter and steeper than the Glade Trail, so it sees more downhill traffic, most often one-way riders from Timberline. Like Glade, it is a safer place when avalanche danger exists higher up. If the snow is good, several runs may be warranted. Since it is shorter and steeper, choose Alpine first, then if you have time do Glade, too. Another option is to combine this trip with a half day of resort skiing or snowboarding.

## Getting There

Drive east on U.S. 26 from Portland 60 miles to Government Camp. Take the second Government Camp exit and park in the sno-park at Summit Ski Area.

Alternatively, a one-way trip starts from Timberline Lodge. The well-marked Timberline Road is a few hundred yards east of Government Camp on U.S. 26. Most one-way snow riders leave a car at Summit Ski Area Sno-park in Government Camp and get a ride to Timberline.

Government Camp, a.k.a. "Govy"

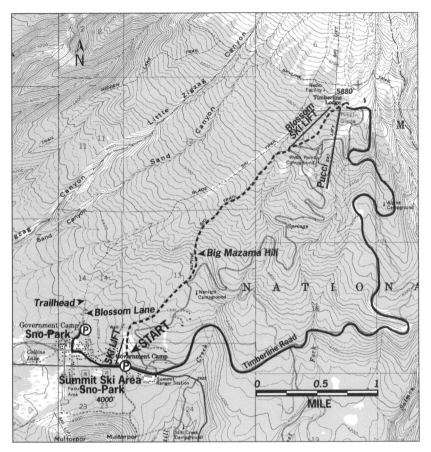

## The Route

From Summit Ski Area, hike up the east flank of the ski run via the West Leg Trail to the top of the chairlift. Stay clear of ski runs and watch for down-hillers. The Alpine Trail starts at the top of and behind the lift. Follow the well-marked trail through the woods. After about 1 mile is a steeper section called Big Mazama Hill. The trail continues through the woods and ends about 2 miles later at the bottom of Blossom lift. Continue hiking up to Timberline Lodge, then turn around and glide down.

From Timberline, make turns down the resort slope marked "Alpine" toward Blossom lift. The Alpine Trail begins at the bottom of Blossom lift and should be marked. Follow signs through the woods and down Big Mazama Hill to Summit Ski Area and Government Camp.

# 4 MOUNT HOOD SOUTH
## Palmer Glacier

❄❄❄

| | |
|---|---|
| Starting point | Timberline Lodge, 5,880 feet |
| High point | Top of Palmer Lift, 8,540 feet |
| Drive distance/time | 70 miles, 1.5 hours |
| Trail distance/time | 4 miles, 3 hours |
| Skill level | Beginner |
| Best season | Spring |
| Maps | USGS Mount Hood South, Geo-Graphics Mount Hood Wilderness |

Palmer Glacier and its lower snowfield make a great place for beginner back-country riders. Because this route is in the ski area, the area is best hiked in the early morning during ski season. Always check with the Timberline ski patrol first. If there are in-area skiers, stay clear of them.

## Getting There

From Portland, drive east on U.S. 26 about 60 miles to Government Camp. Just past Government Camp, turn left onto Timberline Road. After winding 6 miles up the hill, you'll reach Timberline Ski Area. The first parking lot on the right side of the road is the climber's lot.

## The Route

Begin on the snowfield at Timberline Lodge and head more or less straight up the mountain. Stay to the right of the Magic Mile chairlift. The slope is a wide-open, low-angle grade. After about a mile you'll reach the halfway point, Silcox Warming Hut, at 7,016 feet. Continue up the mountain, staying to the right of the Palmer chairlift. The hut at the top of Palmer lift is at 8,540 feet. From there you can get a good view of higher routes and their landmarks, including Illumination Rock, Crater Rock, and the summit.

The ride heads back down the climbing route. The wide-open, low-angle slopes give you plenty of room for turns. Don't climb too late in the day or slush will slow you down significantly. For much of the year, even well into summer, you should be able to make tracks all the way to Timberline Lodge.

Hiking up south side of Mount Hood, with Tom, Dick, and Harry Mountain in background

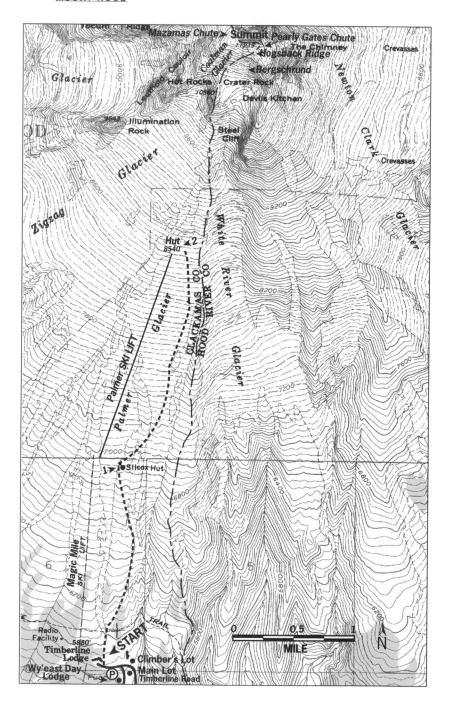

## MOUNT HOOD SOUTH

# 5 Crater Rock

❋ ❋ ❋ ❋

| | |
|---|---|
| Starting point | Timberline Lodge, 5,880 feet |
| High point | Crater Rock, 10,500 feet |
| Drive distance/time | 70 miles, 1.5 hours |
| Trail distance/time | 6 miles, 5 hours |
| Skill level | Intermediate |
| Best season | Spring |
| Maps | USGS Mount Hood South, Geo-Graphics Mount Hood Wilderness |

Crater Rock is perhaps the most popular destination on Hood's south side. It is especially attractive for snow gliders who get a late start in the morning or don't have skill to make the summit of Mount Hood. Some who sleep late even ride the Palmer chairlift and hike to better snow at Crater Rock to make this a super-quick trip. It's a great way to scout the summit route for later in the season.

## Getting There

From Portland, drive east on U.S. 26 about 60 miles to Government Camp. Just past Government Camp, turn left onto Timberline Road. After winding 6

Skinning up Palmer Glacier to Crater Rock, Mount Hood

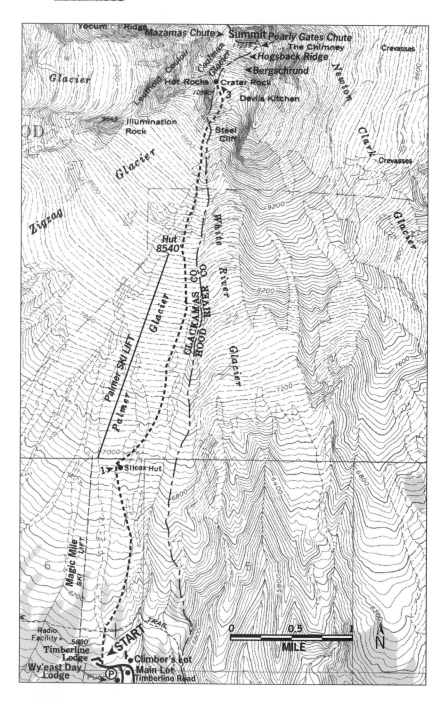

miles up the hill, you'll reach Timberline Ski Area. The first parking lot on the right side of the road is the climber's lot.

## The Route

Begin on the snowfield at Timberline Lodge and head more or less straight up the mountain. Stay to the right of the Magic Mile chairlift. The slope is a wide-open and low-angle grade. After about a mile you'll reach Silcox Warming Hut at 7,016 feet. Continue up the mountain, on a steeper slope, staying just to the right of the Palmer chairlift. In another mile you reach the hut at the top of Palmer lift at 8,540 feet. Continue one-third of a mile up Palmer Glacier to Crater Rock, the large rock at the base of the summit.

The ride heads back down the climbing route. On a clear day you should be able to see the whole route, all the way back to Timberline Lodge. For untracked snow, the best bet is to ride down the slopes, staying just to the rider's right, or north, of the Palmer and Magic Mile lifts. For most of the year, you should be able to make tracks all the way back to Timberline Lodge.

Below Crater Rock, use caution if the weather or visibility is poor. Remain wary of the Mount Hood Triangle (see chapter introduction). If you follow the fall line below Crater Rock, you ride away from Timberline and down the Zigzag Glacier to the Mississippi Head Cliffs. The correct route down is a slight traverse to the rider's left that generally follows magnetic south on a compass.

# 6 Illumination Rock

❄❄❄❄

| | |
|---|---|
| Starting point | Timberline Lodge, 5,880 feet |
| High point | Illumination Rock Saddle, 9,300 feet |
| Drive distance/time | 70 miles, 1.5 hours |
| Trail distance/time | 6 miles, 5 hours |
| Skill level | Intermediate |
| Best season | Spring |
| Maps | USGS Mount Hood South, Geo-Graphics Mount Hood Wilderness |

Illumination Rock is a second tour above Timberline's Palmer chairlift and is similar to the Crater Rock route. Many people skin over to Illumination Rock to get away from the crowded South Climb route. Oftentimes you can find fresh tracks when the slopes below Crater Rock are tracked up.

## Getting There

From Portland, drive east on U.S. 26 about 60 miles to Government Camp. Just past Government Camp, turn left onto Timberline Road. After winding 6 miles up the hill, you'll reach Timberline Ski Area. The first parking lot on the right side of the road is the climber's lot.

Cranking turns in spring corn, south side Mount Hood

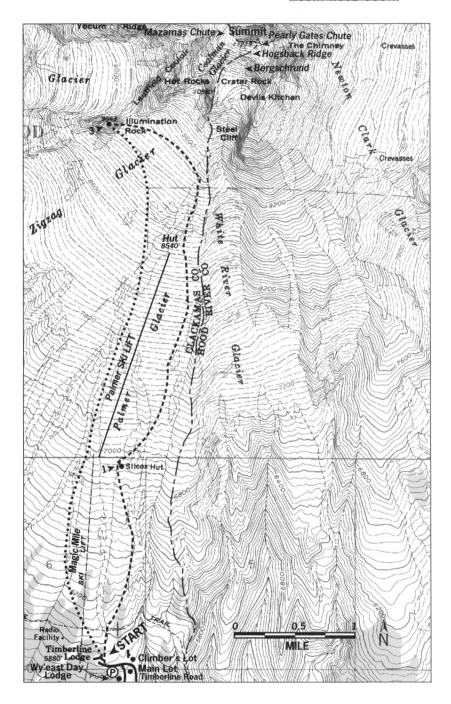

# The Route

Begin on the snowfield at Timberline Lodge and head more or less straight up the mountain. Stay to the right of the Magic Mile chairlift. The slope is a wide-open and low-angle grade. After about a mile you'll reach Silcox Warming Hut at 7,016 feet. Continue up the mountain on a steeper slope, staying to the right of the Palmer chairlift. In another mile you reach the top of Palmer lift at 8,540 feet. Once at the top of the lift, traverse north, or climber's left. Illumination Rock should be visible to the north about a mile away.

The ride heads back down the climbing route. On a clear day you should be able to see the whole route, all the way back to Timberline Lodge. For untracked snow, the best bet is to ride down the slopes, staying just to the rider's right, or north, of the Palmer and Magic Mile lifts. For most of the year, you should be able to make tracks all the way back to Timberline Lodge.

Below Illumination Rock, use caution if the weather or visibility is poor. Remain wary of the Mount Hood Triangle (see chapter introduction). If you follow the fall line below Illumination Rock, you ride away from Timberline and down the Zigzag Glacier to the Mississippi Head Cliffs. The correct route down is a slight traverse to the rider's left that generally follows magnetic south on a compass.

# MOUNT HOOD SOUTH
# South Climb

❄❄❄❄❄

| | |
|---|---|
| Starting point | Timberline Lodge, 5,880 feet |
| High point | Summit, 11,239 feet |
| Drive distance/time | 70 miles, 1.5 hours |
| Trail distance/time | 7 miles, 8 hours |
| Skill level | Advanced |
| Best season | Spring |
| Maps | USGS Mount Hood South, Geo-Graphics Mount Hood Wilderness |

The South Climb is the most popular advanced ski and snowboard mountaineering route in Oregon, if not in the entire Cascades. This route is for expert skiers and snowboarders only. Several additional hazards are on the summit pitch beyond Crater Rock: a steep chute, ice and rock fall, and the bergschrund. The summit pitch should only be ridden in spring when the bergschrund is closed and avalanche danger is at a minimum. Otherwise, a more common practice is to leave your glisse gear at Hogsback Ridge, boot to the summit and back, then ride down from the ridge. If you attempt the summit, be prepared to bring crampons, helmet, ice ax, rope, and pickets.

## Getting There
From Portland, drive east on U.S. 26 about 60 miles to Government Camp. Just past Government Camp, turn left onto Timberline Road. After winding 6

Carving the south side of Mount Hood

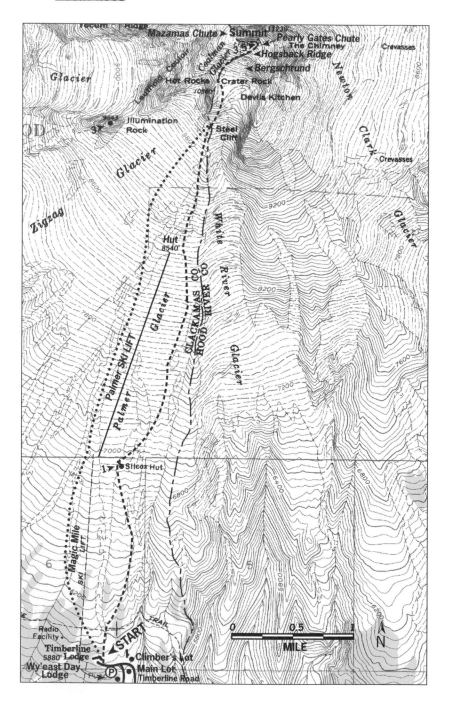

miles up the hill, you'll reach Timberline Ski Area. The first parking lot on the right side of the road is the climber's lot.

## The Route

Begin on the snowfield at Timberline Lodge and head more or less straight up the mountain. Stay to the right of the Magic Mile chairlift. The slope is a wide-open, low-angle grade. After about a mile you'll reach Silcox Warming Hut at 7,016 feet. Continue up the mountain on a steeper slope staying right of the Palmer chairlift. In another mile you reach the top of the Palmer lift at 8,540 feet. Continue about one-third of a mile up Palmer Glacier to Crater Rock, the large rock at the base of the summit.

At Crater Rock skirt around the base to the east, or climber's right, and gain snow-covered Hogsback Ridge. Some parties rope up at this point. Hike along the Hogsback to the final chute, called the Pearly Gates. If the bergschrund is closed, it may be easy to cross. If it is open, you will need to detour a few hundred feet to the east, climber's right, close to the rocks. Watch for falling rock and icefall. Be careful of falling on the final steep pitch through the Pearly Gates. Use an ice ax and crampons. If you are roped, consider using a running belay for safety.

The ride down heads through the steep, narrow Pearly Gates chute, about a 40-degree slope, to the Devil's Kitchen bowl. Watch for climbers coming up the chute and be careful of the bergschrund; you should only ride off the summit when the bergschrund is well-covered. You will probably want to descend with an ice ax or self-arrest grip poles. If you choose to stash your gear at Hogsback Ridge, hike down the way you came up.

The ride down from Crater Rock heads back along the climbing route. On a clear day you should be able to see the whole route, all the way back to Timberline Lodge. For untracked snow, the best bet is to ride down the slopes, staying just to the rider's right, or north, of the Palmer and Magic Mile lifts. For most of the year, you should be able to make tracks all the way back to Timberline Lodge.

Below Crater Rock, use caution if the weather or visibility is poor. Remain wary of the Mount Hood Triangle (see chapter introduction). If you follow the fall line below Crater Rock, you ride away from Timberline and down the Zigzag Glacier to the Mississippi Head Cliffs. The correct route down is a slight traverse to the rider's left that generally follows magnetic south on a compass.

# 8 | West Crater Rim

❄❄❄❄

| | |
|---|---|
| Starting point | Timberline Lodge, 5,880 feet |
| High point | Summit, 11,239 feet |
| Drive distance/time | 70 miles, 1.5 hours |
| Trail distance/time | 7 miles, 8 hours |
| Skill level | Advanced |
| Best season | Spring |
| Maps | USGS Mount Hood South, Geo-Graphics Mount Hood Wilderness |

The West Crater Rim route to the summit is less popular among climbers and glisse mountaineers. It is one step more difficult than the South Climb and probably one of the more difficult and dangerous routes in this book. The summit pitch is marked by a bergschrund and a steep avalanche–prone slope. If the final summit pitch is questionable for a safe ascent or descent, you can always turn around at Crater Rock or backtrack to the South Climb.

South side of Mount Hood from Palmer Lift, Crater Rock in center

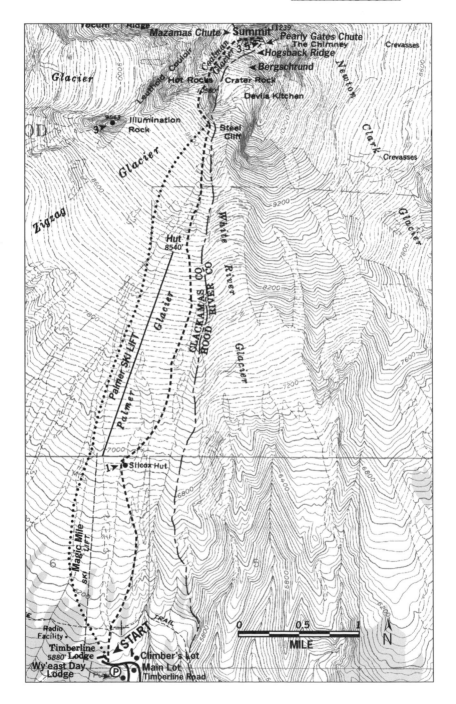

## Getting There

From Portland, drive east on U.S. 26 about 60 miles to Government Camp. Just past Government Camp, turn left onto Timberline Road. After winding 6 miles up the hill, you'll reach Timberline Ski Area. The first parking lot on the right side of the road is the climber's lot.

## The Route

Begin on the snowfield at Timberline Lodge and head more or less straight up the mountain. Stay to the right of the Magic Mile chairlift. The slope is a wide-open, low-angle grade. After about mile you'll reach Silcox Warming Hut at 7,016 feet. Continue up the mountain on a steeper slope staying to the right of the Palmer chairlift. In another mile you reach the top of the Palmer lift at 8,540 feet. Continue about one-third of a mile up Palmer Glacier toward Crater Rock, the large rock at the base of the summit.

Below Crater Rock skirt around to the west, or climber's left. Climb past Hot Rocks and continue up the steep face to the summit. Nearing the top you will gain a flat shelf on Coalman Glacier. Depending on the time of year, you will probably hike over or around the bergschrund. You may have to skirt around it to the west, or climber's left. The final few hundred feet climb through Old Chute or Mazama Chute. When climbing this final pitch, be careful of a fall, avalanches, and falling rock or ice. Most parties rope up, and you should consider using a running belay. Usually crampons and an ice ax are necessary.

The ride down starts at the summit and goes through the 40-degree Old Chute. Watch for climbers coming up the chute and be careful of a fall. You may want to descend with an ice ax or self-arrest grip poles. If in doubt, hike down.

The ride down from Crater Rock heads back along the climbing route. On a clear day you should be able to see the whole route, all the way back to Timberline Lodge. For untracked snow, the best bet is to ride down the slopes, staying just to the rider's right, or north, of the Palmer and Magic Mile lifts. For most of the year, you should be able to make tracks all the way back to Timberline Lodge.

Below Crater Rock, use caution if the weather or visibility is poor. Remain wary of the Mount Hood Triangle (see chapter introduction). If you follow the fall line below Crater Rock, you ride away from Timberline and down the Zigzag Glacier to the Mississippi Head Cliffs. The correct route down is a slight traverse to the rider's left that generally follows magnetic south on a compass.

# 9 Salmon River Canyon

❄❄

| | |
|---|---|
| Starting point | Timberline Lodge, 5,880 feet |
| High point | Silcox Warming Hut, 7,016 feet |
| Drive distance/time | 70 miles, 1.5 hours |
| Trail distance/time | 2 miles, 2 hours |
| Skill level | Beginner |
| Best season | Winter |
| Maps | USGS Mount Hood South, Geo-Graphics Mount Hood Wilderness |

Salmon River Canyon is a popular short route in winter, especially when the snow is poor at lower elevation and the weather is lousy high up. The canyon terrain is not steep, so it is best ridden with fresh, dry snow or spring corn. This is a good beginner route that is close to the ski area and has mellow terrain. Although avalanche danger is low, watch for slides from cornices and small terrain traps.

## Getting There

From Portland, drive east on U.S. 26 about 60 miles to Government Camp. Just past Government Camp, turn left onto Timberline Road. After winding 6

Observe all traction advisories

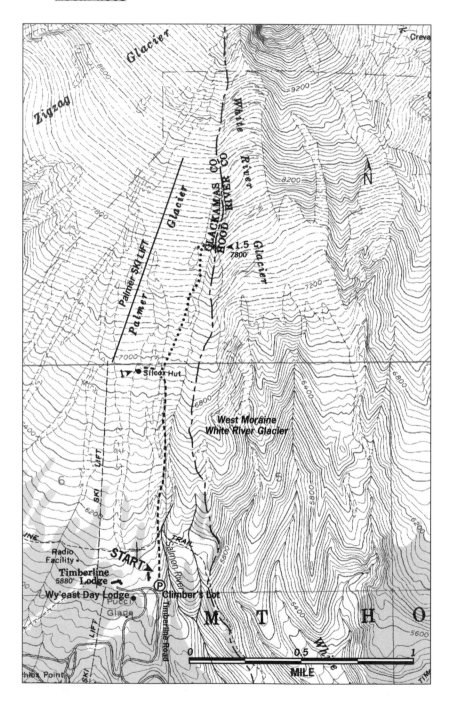

miles up the hill, you'll reach Timberline Ski Area. The first parking lot on the right side of the road is the climber's lot.

## The Route

Unlike most routes that start from Timberline Lodge, the Salmon River Canyon route begins a few hundred feet down the road from the day lodge at the backcountry parking lot. At the north end of the parking lot, climb up the snowbank to the left. Once above the parking lot, climb up the drainage and gain the west ridge on climber's left. After a few hundred feet in trees, the slope opens with shallow gullies on both sides. Follow the drainage up to its terminus at about 7,500 feet near Silcox Warming Hut, the small shelter at the edge of the ski area.

The descent follows the route you took up, usually on the flat, open slopes below Silcox Warming Hut. About halfway down, the slope narrows to a few gullies, then scattered trees. During most of the winter and spring, you should be able to ride down to the parking lot. If weather is poor, use caution when returning to the parking lot: The snowbank on the edge may be tall and sheer from a winter of plowing.

# 10 White River/West Moraine

❄❄

| | |
|---|---|
| Starting point | Timberline Lodge, 5,880 feet |
| High point | White River moraine, 7,800 feet |
| Drive distance/time | 70 miles, 1.5 hours |
| Trail distance/time | 3 miles, 3 hours |
| Skill level | Intermediate |
| Best season | Winter, spring |
| Maps | USGS Mount Hood South, Geo-Graphics Mount Hood Wilderness |

White River Canyon is a less popular tour from Timberline but accessible in the winter when lower slopes don't have good snow and high slopes are too dangerous. The terrain is for the most part mellow, but some steep shots can be found. Although the route is close to the ski area, you will be separated from it by several gullies, hence it is a good wilderness experience.

## Getting There

From Portland, drive east on U.S. 26 about 60 miles to Government Camp. Just past Government Camp, turn left onto Timberline Road. After winding 6 miles up the hill, you'll reach Timberline Ski Area. The first parking lot on the right side of the road is the climber's lot.

Snowboard ascent gear: crampons, ice ax, snowshoes, self-arrest poles, firn gliders, skins

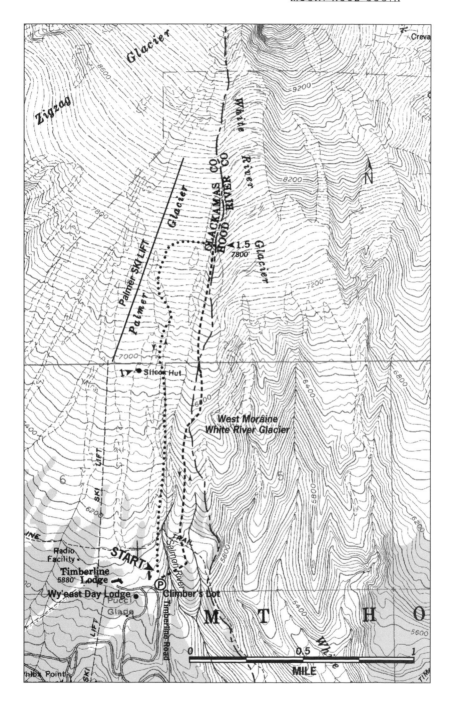

## The Route

Like Salmon River Canyon, the Upper White River Canyon route begins at the climber's parking lot. At the north end of the parking lot, the canyon is the large drainage system to the east, or climber's right.

To start, skin or snowshoe down the first small drainage, then back up to a broad, flat ridge that is east of the parking lot. The route follows this ridge, the west moraine of the White River Glacier, north up the mountain among sparse trees on gentle slopes. Be cautious of the steep slopes that fall away to the east to the deep chasm of the glacier and headwaters of the White River. You may want to hike over for a look, but don't get too close.

Follow the ridge up through small glades, gullies, and, once beyond the trees, windswept rock ridges. About halfway up, skin or snowshoe down a hundred feet or so to gain the next rocky ridge. More ambitious riders may choose to keep going, but much higher than 7,500 feet you will begin to run into crevasses.

The descent affords a couple of options. You can ride the gentle slopes you climbed up or stay in one of the gullies, provided avalanche danger is low and the cornices are not large or unstable. Once down near treeline, watch for the trail you ascended from the parking lot. Around 6,000 feet, ride down the small drainage and hike up to the parking lot.

Another option is to traverse from around 7,800 feet to Timberline Ski Area and Silcox Warming Hut, then ride the gentle slopes below Silcox down to the parking lot.

## MOUNT HOOD SOUTH

# 11 Boy Scout Ridge

❄❄

| | |
|---|---|
| Starting point | White River West Sno-park, 4,200 feet |
| High point | Boy Scout Ridge, 6,000 feet |
| Drive distance/time | 70 miles, 2 hours |
| Trail distance/time | 5 miles, 2 hours |
| Skill level | Beginner |
| Best season | Winter |
| Maps | USGS Mount Hood South, Geo-Graphics Mount Hood Wilderness |

Boy Scout Ridge is the lower section of the West Moraine of White River Canyon (see White River/West Moraine). This is an excellent beginner route that starts at the White River West Sno-park and goes to Timberline. However, many downhillers prefer to ride one-way only from Timberline Lodge by using a car shuttle. It can be combined with the upper White River route for a longer tour. Lower White River Canyon is popular among cross-country skiers, snowshoers, and sledders, mostly because it is incredibly beautiful and accessible.

White River from Boy Scout Ridge, Mount Hood

## Getting There

From Portland, drive east on U.S. 26 about 60 miles to Government Camp. About 3 miles past Government Camp follow signs to Oregon 35 north toward Hood River. In about 5 more miles park at the White River West Sno-park on the left.

## The Route

From the far end of the parking lot, start north along the river bottom on a ski trail. In a half mile, you come to a small open slope called the "Bowl" or "Gravel Pit." Climb the small slope to the bench above the river and continue on the broad, gentle slope through the trees. At about 5,000 feet you will

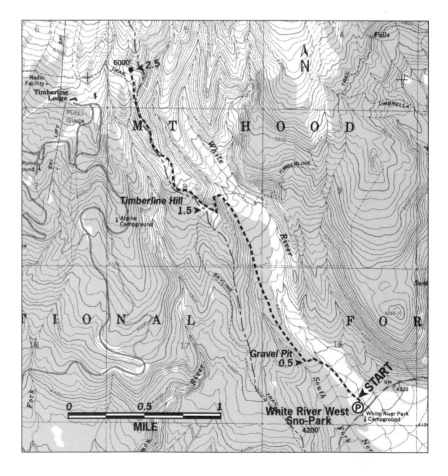

come to the tree line. Ascend the short but steep slope to the left and continue up the ridge.

Once at timberline, continue up the broad, open ridge. You will see Timberline Lodge to the left. Be cautious of the steep slopes that fall away to the east. For a longer tour, continue up the west moraine (see White River/West Moraine).

To descend, follow the gentle slope you came up. Once down near the tree line, watch for the trail you climbed up. You can reach the White River by descending back down the steep slope to 5,000 feet. If you drop down to the valley floor, you may need to cross and recross the braided channel of the river, which may or may not be covered by more snow bridges. From the Gravel Pit, it may be a rough ride back to the parking lot with snowshoe, sled, and cross-country ski tracks everywhere. Because the route is pretty flat, snowboarders probably will want to use poles.

# 12 Skylar Bowl

❄❄❄❄❄

| | |
|---|---|
| Starting point | White River West Sno-park, 4,200 feet |
| High point | Skylar Bowl, 8,200 feet |
| Drive distance/time | 70 miles, 2 hours |
| Trail distance/time | 8 miles, 6 hours |
| Skill level | Beginner to advanced |
| Best season | Winter |
| Maps | USGS Mount Hood South, Geo-Graphics Mount Hood Wilderness |

Skylar Bowl is in White River Canyon, the huge drainage between Timberline and Mount Hood Meadows Ski Areas. Flanked by Boy Scout Ridge and the west moraine on one side and Cascade River on the other, it is a large and incredibly beautiful glacier drainage. A breathtaking view of Mount Hood and spectacular moraines make this an awesome tour. Some other key elements also make this a wonderful touring locale. First, Skylar Bowl is a large area, with numerous slopes on the moraines in the White River Canyon; there is something for everyone, from low-angle to steeps. (Because

Looking into White River from Cascade Ridge, Mount Hood

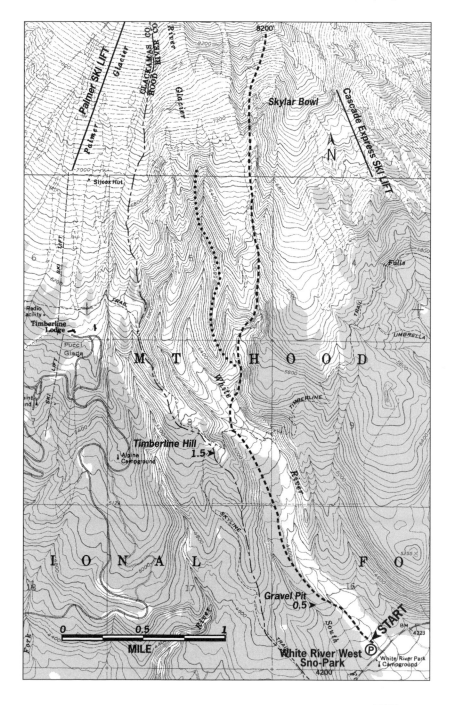

all slopes have the same approach and are close to each other, they are described as one route.) Second, Skylar Bowl is in the sun all day, so the corn often provides excellent riding here when slopes are bulletproof and wind-blown higher on the mountain. On the same note, powder is prevalent when it is all tracked up in resorts. Third, the bowl can be accessed from the ski areas to make approach easier. At the time of this writing, only Timberline allowed out-of-bounds travel.

The main risks of this area are threefold: the creek, which may or may not be covered by snow bridges, which may or may not be stable; avalanches that are frequent on the steep upper slopes; and crevasses that mark the beginning of the White River Glacier at the head of the canyon.

## Getting There

From Portland, drive east on U.S. 26 about 60 miles to Government Camp. About 3 miles past Government Camp follow signs to Oregon 35 north toward Hood River. In about 5 more miles park on the left at the White River West Sno-park. There is another lot, White River East, across the bridge on the right-hand side.

## The Route

From the far end of the parking lot, start north along the river bottom on a ski trail. In a half mile, you come to a small open slope called the "Gravel Pit." Continue another mile up the river to timberline. From here you will see huge moraines and numerous options.

Most people hike up the east side, a steep slope that continues up to Cas-cade Ridge at Mount Hood Meadows. It has a great fall line and faces south. Another option is the large moraine in the center of the canyon. On the cen-ter moraine, usually the east-facing or south-facing slope has the best snow. The west side can be hard and windblown in winter, and is very steep.

On the way out, head down the way you came in, making tracks down the slope you ascended, then skiing or snowboarding out the flats for the last mile. From timberline, it may be a rough ride back to the parking lot with snowshoe, sled, and cross-country ski tracks everywhere. Because it is pretty flat, snowboarders probably will want to use poles. Watch the snow bridges.

# 13 Wy'east Face (from White River)

❄❄❄❄

| | |
|---|---|
| Starting point | White River West Sno-park, 4,200 feet |
| High point | Wy'east Face, 10,500 feet |
| Drive distance/time | 70 miles, 1.5 hours |
| Trail distance/time | 8 miles, 8 hours |
| Skill level | Advanced |
| Best season | Spring |
| Maps | USGS Mount Hood South, Geo-Graphics Mount Hood Wilderness |

The Wy'east Face is a classic late spring or early summer descent. It rivals Snowdome on the north side for sheer riding pleasure. Wy'east Face is very accessible. There are several ways to get to the Wy'east by hiking or utilizing chairlifts. Be cautious, however, as this is a serious ski or snowboard mountaineering trip. At the very least, you should be skilled at mountaineering and should have summitted Mount Hood from the south side. The best ride is on spring corn, early in the day to minimize avalanche danger. The route affords

White River drainage, Wy'east Face on right, Mount Hood

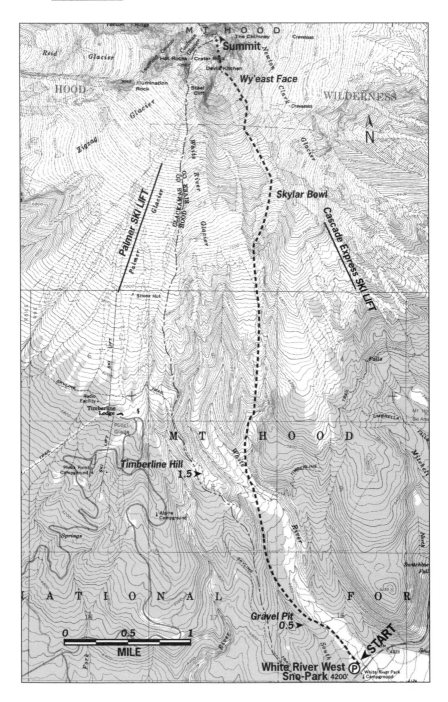

beautiful views, excellent south-facing snow, and few crowds. Watch for the White River snow bridges, crevasses that mark the beginning of the White River Glacier at the head of the canyon, and avalanche danger. Also, because the face is steep, a fall could send you sliding for your life. It can also be climbed from the east; see Route 21.

## Getting There

From Portland, drive east on U.S. 26 about 60 miles to Government Camp. About 3 miles past Government Camp follow signs to Oregon 35 north toward Hood River. In about 5 miles park on the left at the White River West Sno-park.

## The Route

From the far end of the parking lot, start north along the river bottom on a ski trail. In a half mile, you come to a small open slope, the "Gravel Pit." Skin up the flats another mile upriver to timberline. Then continue due north up a snowfield, Skylar Bowl; this bowl is between the crevasses of the White River Glacier and Cascade Ridge in Mount Hood Meadows. The Wy'east Face will be in full view. At the top of Skylar Bowl, you will be at the bottom of Wy'east Face, around 9,000 feet. You will be at the junction of Heather Canyon and White River Canyon, just above the Cascade lift at Mount Hood Meadows.

Climb to the top of the Wy'east Face only if snow conditions are favorable and avalanche danger is at a minimum. You definitely will need an ice ax and helmet; you may need crampons early in the day, too. Most climbers stay to the left of the face. At the top, a short hike on the ridge above Steel Cliff takes you to the summit, but it is not skiable. Attempt this only if you are properly equipped and skilled.

On descent, head directly down the Wy'east Face, the Skylar Bowl snow-field, and White River Canyon. This 6,000-foot descent is a blast, providing the snow is good. On the way out, make turns down the way you came in, then ski or snowboard out the flats for the last mile.

# Mount Hood East

The southeast and east sides of Mount Hood can provide some of the best winter backcountry snow riding in Northern Oregon. The snow stays a bit drier and the sky is a bit sunnier when compared to Timberline and the south side. This corner of the mountain is dominated by Mount Hood Meadows Ski Resort and includes a large area: The Cascade Express lift and snowcat skiing take resort snow riders to nearly 8,000 feet; Heather Canyon comes down to about 4,000 feet and includes both downhillers and cross-country skiers.

Winter access is via two main sno-parks, Mount Hood Meadows and Hood River Meadows. Many of the tours on this side are partially or entirely in-area. These routes provide some early winter riding before the resort opens. To date, lift-access backcountry touring is not allowed, although it would make for great tours. If you hike during the season, hike from the parking lot and steer clear of skiers. In midwinter, it may be crowded here, especially when you're competing with downhill skiers and snowboarders for Superbowl or with Nordic skiers in lower Heather Canyon.

Spring skiing can be great here, especially in April and May when the snow is still plentiful. The approach up the ski resort is easy and crowd-free when the resort is closed on weekdays in spring. This is a good place to tour to avoid the south-side crowds and when the road to Cooper Spur road on the north side is still closed.

## Mount Hood East Maps

USFS Mount Hood Wilderness, Geo-Graphics Mount Hood Wilderness, Green Trails Mount Hood 462

## Primary Info Centers/Ranger Districts

Mount Hood National Forest Headquarters, Portland, OR: 503/668-1700, www.fs.fed.us/r6/mthood

Hood River Ranger District: 541/622-3191

## Avalanche/Weather/Road Conditions

Northwest Weather and Avalanche Center: 503/808-2400, www.nwac.noaa.gov

National Weather Service: 503/261-9246 or 360/694-6136, www.nws.noaa.gov

Oregon DOT Pass Report: 800/977-6368, www.odot.state.or.us/roads

# Ski Area Snow Reports

Mount Hood Meadows, 503/227-7669, www.skihood.com

## Permits

A wilderness permit and climber's registration are required for climbing in the Mount Hood Wilderness, which is on the east side above about 9,000 feet. For the most part, this includes the Wy'east Face and Newton Creek drainage. These self-issued permits are available at the ranger stations or at Timberline's Wy'east Day Lodge.

A sno-park pass is required from November 15 to April 30.

## Of Special Note

Since most of these runs are partially or entirely within Mount Hood Meadows Ski Area, they are best ridden before the resort is open for the season or when it is closed in spring. At the time of this writing, lift-access backcountry riding is not allowed. Check with the ski patrol to get the current regulations. If you hike during the season, start early from the parking lot, stay on the edge of the runs, and watch for downhill skiers and snowboarders.

## MOUNT HOOD EAST

# 14 | Meadows Bowls

❄❄

| | |
|---|---|
| Starting point | Mount Hood Meadows, 5,360 feet |
| High point | One Bowl, 6,400 feet |
| Drive distance/time | 70 miles, 1.5 hours |
| Trail distance/time | 2 miles, 2 hours |
| Skill level | Beginner |
| Best season | Fall |
| Maps | USGS Mount Hood South, Geo-Graphics Mount Hood Wilderness |

This fairly straightforward hike is another good place for beginners to start. Because it is in the ski area, this route is perhaps at its best in late fall during the week before the resort opens for the season. In spring you will find lots of snow but it will likely be hard-packed or crud from the resort skiers and snowboarders. Depending on snow, hike as early as October or as late as December. Because so many people get the early-season Joneses, it may be fairly crowded.

## Getting There

From Portland, drive east on U.S. 26 about 60 miles through Government Camp. About 3 miles past Government Camp follow signs to Oregon 35 north toward Hood River. After 7 more miles turn left on the Mount Hood Meadows road.

## The Route

From the Mount Hood Meadows parking lot, walk around the main lodge. The route follows the Mount Hood Express lift line up the mountain. On the lower section, stay near the trees under the lift for avalanche safety and to preserve as much snow as possible for the trip down. After a thousand feet, you come to a bench where you will have a good view of the bowls. Bowl One is under and just to the hiker's left of the lift. Bowls Two, Three, and Four wrap around counterclockwise. If you have time, hike to the top of Bowl One or Two for the most vertical. Bowl Three is not as far but offers good turns.

Bowl Four is the shortest hike, about 1,000 feet lower than the others and almost out of sight from the Mount Hood Express lift. It is easier to hike to

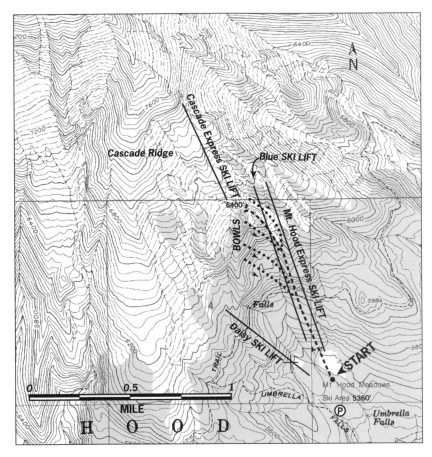

Bowl Four along the Blue lift line. It can also be accessed by hiking up the Daisy lift line. At the bottom of Bowl Four is a flat section through the trees where snowboarders may get bogged down before coming out to the bottom of the Blue lift.

When hiking the bowls, stay close to the trees and watch for avalanche danger. If many people are hiking, watch that someone above you doesn't kick a slide down. If the snow is good, make a few trips back to the top or ride all four.

# 15 Cascade Ridge

❄ ❄ ❄

| | |
|---|---|
| **Starting point** | Mount Hood Meadows, 5,360 feet |
| **High point** | Cascade Ridge, 7,800 feet |
| **Drive distance/time** | 70 miles, 1.5 hours |
| **Trail distance/time** | 4 miles, 3 hours |
| **Skill level** | Beginner |
| **Best season** | Spring |
| **Maps** | USGS Mount Hood South, Geo-Graphics Mount Hood Wilderness |

Cascade Ridge is a long, low-angle route that is great for those just getting to know the southeast side of Hood. It offers scenic vistas of White River Glacier and Canyon since it is actually the upper portion of the east moraine. Because the run is in-area, the snow may be skied out unless you time your trip after a late spring snowfall; in fall there may be sparse cover down low, making the slog to and from the ridge less attractive. Weekdays in April or May when the resort closes are perhaps the best time to get decent snow and avoid the resort snow riders.

## Getting There

From Portland, drive east on U.S. 26 about 60 miles through Government Camp. About 3 miles past Government Camp follow signs to Oregon 35

Hiking above the A-Zone, Mount Hood

north toward Hood River. After 7 more miles turn left on the Mount Hood Meadows road.

## The Route

From the north end of the lodge, hike up the gentle slopes of the Daisy lift to the bottom of Cascade Express, staying close to the trees. Once up near tree line, hike to the treed ridge to the left and west of the lift. If the weather is poor, it is easy to get disoriented above the treeline, so you may consider heading down from there. Otherwise, follow the ridge to the left of Cascade Express lift to the top of the lift.

To descend, follow one of several runs near the Cascade Express lift, either the bowl near the lift or the west ridge. At the bottom of the Cascade Express lift, follow the Daisy lift line back to the main lodge and parking areas.

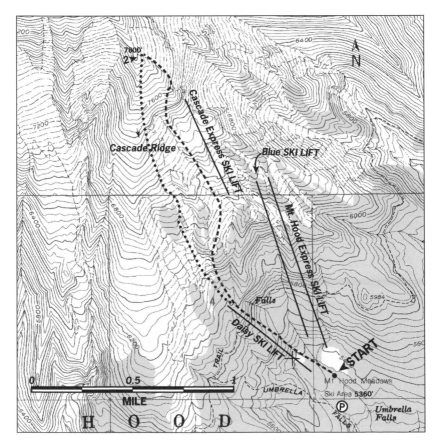

# 16 Lower Heather Canyon

❄ ❄ ❄

| | |
|---|---|
| Starting point | Hood River Meadows, 4,520 feet |
| High point | Heather Canyon, 6,000 feet |
| Drive distance/time | 70 miles, 1.5 hours |
| Trail distance/time | 3 miles, 2 hours |
| Skill level | Beginner |
| Best season | Winter |
| Maps | USGS Mount Hood South, Geo-Graphics Mount Hood Wilderness |

Lower Heather Canyon is a good beginner or intermediate trip with so many different slopes that it can be skied again and again. Since it is low in elevation, it is best attempted in midwinter or early spring. Because it is part of Mount Hood Meadows, check access rules before heading up the canyon. Also, early or late in the season the stream may not be snow-covered and it may be difficult to cross; if so, be prepared to ford it.

## Getting There

From Portland, drive east on U.S. 26 about 60 miles through Government Camp. About 3 miles past Government Camp follow signs to Oregon 35 north toward Hood River. After 7 more miles pass the Mount Hood Meadows road. Continue another mile and turn left on the Hood River Meadows road.

## The Route

From the Hood River Meadows parking lot, take the Heather Canyon ski trail that follows the Clark Creek drainage. Resort skiers and snowboarders may be coming down, and cross-country skiers may be going up this nearly flat approach during the resort season. Follow the trail about 2 miles until the canyon opens up at about 5,500 feet.

From there you can ride any of many shots at timberline. The north side, called Jill's Woods, is best because it is not accessible by resort snow riders. The south slopes are gentler and have more trees. If you are more ambitious, continue up the canyon above the tree line to around 6,500 or 7,000 feet for drier, deeper snow. Because the slopes are steep and open, use caution to avoid avalanches; sometimes Heather Canyon is closed to resort snow riders because of avalanche danger. Stick to ridges and trees. Check conditions before you go.

Make several runs if the snow is good. When you reach your time or energy limit, head back down the gentle ski trail to the parking lot.

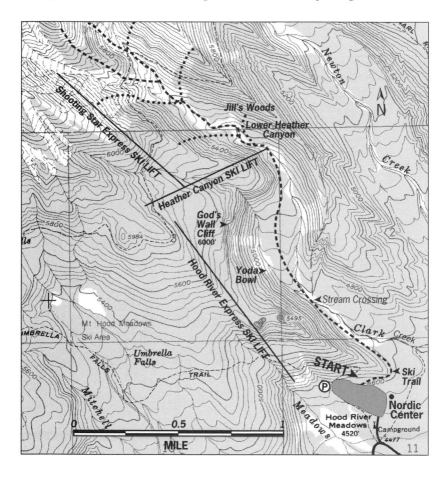

## 17 | MOUNT HOOD EAST
# Yoda Bowl
❄ ❄ ❄

| | |
|---|---|
| Starting point | Hood River Meadows, 4,520 feet |
| High point | Yoda Bowl, 6,000 feet |
| Drive distance/time | 70 miles, 1.5 hours |
| Trail distance/time | 1 mile, 1 hour |
| Skill level | Intermediate |
| Best season | Winter |
| Maps | USGS Mount Hood South, Geo-Graphics Mount Hood Wilderness |

Yoda Bowl is a little shot in the woods of lower Heather Canyon. Like Tom, Dick, and Harry Mountain, it is good for a half-day venture or combined with another tour. It is found just above Hood River Meadows, the lower parking lot of the resort, but outside the ski area boundary. It suffers from low elevation, so it gets the most traffic in midwinter after a storm. Beware: It is steep and avalanche potential is high.

## Getting There

From Portland, drive east on U.S. 26 about 60 miles through Government Camp. About 3 miles past Government Camp follow signs to Oregon 35 north toward Hood River. After 7 more miles, you will pass the Mount Hood Meadows road. Continue another mile and turn left on the Hood River Meadows road.

## The Route

From the Hood River Meadows parking lot, start up the Heather Canyon ski trail. After a half mile and 20 minutes of hiking, you will see the bowl to the left. After the ski trail crosses a bridge over Clark Creek, you will have to cross snow bridges over stream channels, so use caution. Veer up into the trees and to the base of the bowl. Hike to the top, staying in or near the thick woods. Watch the cliff at the top, God's Wall, for skiers and snowboarders ducking ski-area boundaries to poach the bowl.

At the bottom of the bowl, hike or skin back out the Heather Canyon ski trail.

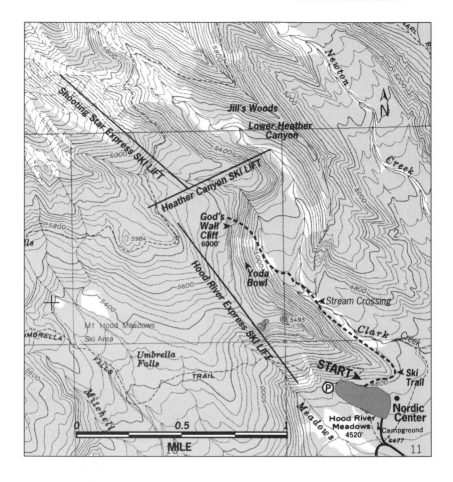

## MOUNT HOOD EAST
# 18 Superbowl (from Mount Hood Meadows)

❄❄❄❄❄

| | |
|---|---|
| Starting point | Mount Hood Meadows, 5,360 feet |
| High point | Superbowl, 8,400 feet |
| Drive distance/time | 70 miles, 1.5 hours |
| Trail distance/time | 5 miles, 4 hours |
| Skill level | Advanced |
| Best season | Spring |
| Maps | USGS Mount Hood South, Geo-Graphics Mount Hood Wilderness |

Superbowl is an outrageous ride when the weather and snow cooperate. Some of this route has tremendous avalanche danger most of the winter, so choose your day wisely to attempt this one. It is within Mount Hood Meadows Ski Area, despite not having lift access to the top. In winter, it is accessed by in-area skiers by hiking above the Cascade Express lift or via a snowcat service.

The best combination of snow and weather, not to mention the best opportunity to avoid lift-access skiers and snowboarders, occurs in April or

Heather Canyon and Superbowl from treeline, Mount Hood

52

May, when the resort is closed on weekdays. Go on a clear, sunny day of spring corn. Because access is significantly different from the two sno-parks, I describe two separate approaches and descents. See also Route 19.

## Getting There

From Portland, drive east on U.S. 26 about 60 miles through Government Camp. About 3 miles past Government Camp follow signs to Oregon 35 north toward Hood River. After 7 more miles turn onto the Mount Hood Meadows road.

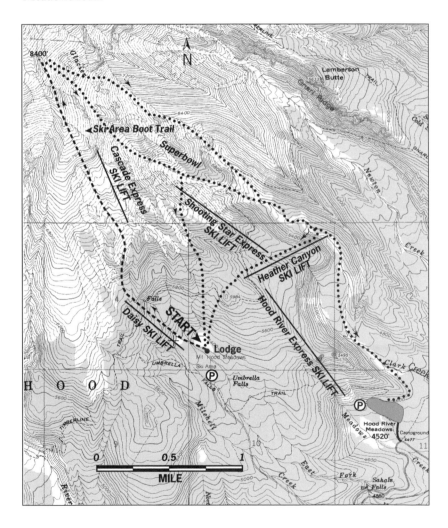

## The Route

From the north end of the lodge, hike up the gentle slopes of the Daisy lift to the bottom of Cascade Express, staying close to the trees. Once up near the tree line, hike to the treed ridge to the left and west of the lift, the east moraine of White River. At the top of the Cascade Express lift, continue up the ridgeline where the slope steepens. If the snow is firm or slick, it may be easier hiking up the rocks. About 1,000 feet above the top of the lift, you will be at a saddle that looks down to Superbowl.

When the resort is open, it allows access to Superbowl via a boot track above "A Zone," which is just east of the top of the Cascade Express lift.

To descend, head down the huge wide bowl, taking any one of several lines, some of which are steep. One section down the middle is the obvious, easy way down. When into the canyon, make turns down to about 6,000 feet; from here three options lead back to the parking lot.

First, you can hike or skin up to the Shooting Star Ridge and the top of Shooting Star Express lift. This allows you to ride back down the ski resort runs to the main lodge and the parking area. A second option continues down Heather Canyon to the bottom of the Heather Canyon lift at about 5,200 feet. Hike the Heather Canyon lift line to the top and ride down to the main parking lot. A third option continues down the flat runout of Heather Canyon to Hood River Meadows Sno-park. But be advised that the lower reaches of the canyon may not have much snow in the spring. And don't count on a ride back to the top if the resort is closed; it's a long walk.

# 19

## Superbowl (from Hood River Meadows)

❄❄❄❄❄

| | |
|---|---|
| Starting point | Hood River Meadows, 4,520 feet |
| High point | Superbowl, 8,400 feet |
| Drive distance/time | 70 miles, 1.5 hours |
| Trail distance/time | 4 miles, 5 hours |
| Skill level | Advanced |
| Best season | Spring |
| Maps | USGS Mount Hood South, Geo-Graphics Mount Hood Wilderness |

The second route to Superbowl via Heather Canyon is longer, although hiking among the occasional crowds of Heather Canyon can be more of a problem than the distance. However, if you need to check the route and snow conditions on the way up, this is the preferred route. If you have a full day and lots of daylight, this is a scenic, rewarding trip that gives you a killer workout, too. See also Route 18.

## Getting There

From Portland, drive east on U.S. 26 about 60 miles through Government Camp. About 3 miles past Government Camp follow signs to Oregon 35 north toward Hood River. After 7 more miles, you will pass the Mount Hood Meadows road. Continue another mile and turn left on the Hood River Meadows road.

## The Route

From the Hood River Meadows parking lot, take the Heather Canyon ski trail that follows the Clark Creek drainage. Follow the trail about 2 miles until the canyon opens up at about 5,500 feet. Once Heather Canyon opens above timberline, continue up the right or left drainage. Hike all the way up the face of Superbowl to around 8,400 feet for an excellent view of all the routes and the opportunity to check conditions. Watch for avalanche hazards. You will be fairly exposed in Superbowl, with no islands of safety.

Alternatively, once at 5,500 feet climb the west ridge of the canyon, Shooting Star Ridge, through the trees. Once on this ridge, hike toward the mountain to the top of the Shooting Star Express lift. Continue on this ridge,

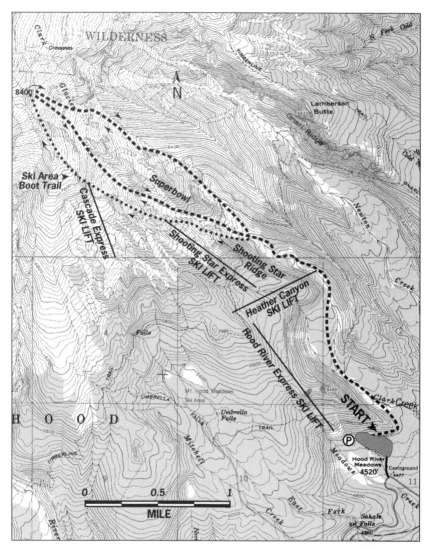

heading northwest for a few hours to the top of Cascade Express. From the top of Cascade Express, continue up another 1,000 feet to a saddle that looks down to Superbowl.

The descent, as in the previous route, can follow any one of several open bowls. Take the 4,000-foot descent in several legs all the way down the canyon and out.

# 20 | Newton Creek

❄❄❄

| | |
|---|---|
| **Starting point** | Hood River Meadows, 4,520 feet |
| **High point** | Pea Gravel Ridge, 5,500 feet |
| **Drive distance/time** | 70 miles, 1.5 hours |
| **Trail distance/time** | 3 miles, 5 hours |
| **Skill level** | Advanced |
| **Best season** | Winter |
| **Maps** | USGS Mount Hood South, Geo-Graphics Mount Hood Wilderness |

Newton Creek is a huge, rarely visited drainage between Heather Canyon and Cooper Spur. It is framed by Pea Gravel Ridge to the south and Gnarl Ridge to the north. Several routes access the drainage, including the Elk Meadows cross-country ski trail. However, skinning up Heather Canyon and over Pea Gravel Ridge seems to be the easiest and most common option for glisse alpinists.

## Getting There

From Portland, drive east on U.S. 26 about 60 miles through Government Camp. About 3 miles past Government Camp follow signs to Oregon 35 north toward Hood River. After 7 more miles, you will pass the Mount Hood Meadows road. Continue another mile and turn left on the Hood River Meadows road.

## The Route

From the Hood River Meadows parking lot, take the Heather Canyon cross-country ski trail that follows the Clark Creek drainage. Follow the trail about 2 miles until the canyon opens up at about 5,000 feet. Climb north up Pea Gravel Ridge at timberline through the sparse trees known as Jill's Woods. Use caution and stick to the trees as this slope is steep. You can also gain the ridge before timberline through the thick woods and rolling snowdrifts called "Potato Patch." The latter is a more difficult climb because of the snowdrifts and tight trees.

Once on Pea Gravel Ridge, descend the slope to Newton Creek, staying close to the trees and watching for avalanche danger. This is the most accessi-

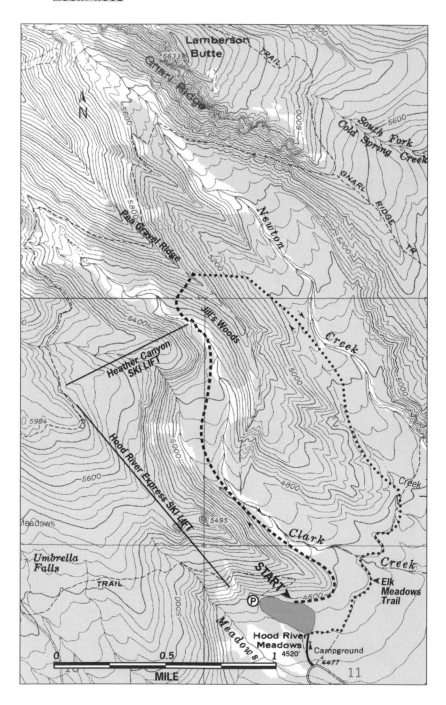

ble slope, but many options exist. Hike the opposite wall, Gnarl Ridge, for spring corn down the chutes. Continue up the canyon to numerous slopes above 5,000 feet. Plan to spend the whole day if you have time. Climb back up to the top of Pea Gravel Ridge for several runs.

The easiest way back out is to climb back up to Pea Gravel and ride back down Heather Canyon. Alternatively, continue down the flat bottom of Newton Creek and catch the Elk Meadows cross-country ski trail back to Hood River Meadows. Be careful you don't miss the trail, especially if you didn't come up this way. This trail is relatively slow. Also, there may be some stream crossings if the snow has melted.

## MOUNT HOOD EAST

# 21 Wy'east Face (from Hood River Meadows)

❄❄❄❄

| | |
|---|---|
| **Starting point** | Hood River Meadows, 4,520 feet |
| **High point** | Wy'east Face, 10,500 feet |
| **Drive distance/time** | 70 miles, 1.5 hours |
| **Trail distance/time** | 6 miles, 6 hours |
| **Skill level** | Advanced |
| **Best season** | Late Spring, summer |
| **Maps** | USGS Mount Hood South, Geo-Graphics Mount Hood Wilderness |

The second route to Wy'east Face is via Heather Canyon and it's a bit longer than from White River; for another alternative, see Route 13. Although Wy'east Face is a classic late spring or early summer descent, it can be dangerous. It is an expert ski and snowboard mountaineering route. You should be skilled at mountaineering and at a minimum should have summitted Mount Hood from the south side. The best ride is on spring corn, early in the day to minimize avalanche danger. You will find beautiful views, excellent south-facing snow, and few crowds. Avalanche danger in Heather Canyon and on

The Wy'east Face from Cascade Ridge, Mount Hood

Wy'east Face is of paramount concern. Also, because the face is steep, a fall could send you sliding for your life.

## Getting There

From Portland, drive east on U.S. 26 about 60 miles through Government Camp. About 3 miles past Government Camp follow signs to Oregon 35 north toward Hood River. After 7 more miles pass the Mount Hood Meadows road. Continue one more mile and turn left on the Hood River Meadows road. Wy'east can also be climbed via Mount Hood Meadows, but that route is not described here.

## The Route

From the Hood River Meadows parking lot, take the Heather Canyon ski trail that follows the Clark Creek drainage. Follow the trail about 2 miles until the canyon opens up at about 5,500 feet. Once Heather Canyon opens above timberline, continue up the right or left drainage. Hike all the way up the face of Superbowl to around 8,400 feet. This will give you an excellent view of all the routes and the ability to check conditions. Watch for avalanche hazards. You will be fairly exposed in Superbowl, especially to falling rock and icefall and resort riders, and there are no islands of safety.

Alternatively, climb the west ridge of the canyon, Shooting Star Ridge, through the trees. Once on this ridge, hike toward the mountain to the top of the Shooting Star Express lift. Continue on this ridge, heading northwest for a few hours to the top of Cascade Express lift. From the top of Cascade Express, continue up another 1,000 feet to a saddle that looks down to Superbowl.

From 8,400 feet, climb to the top of Wy'east Face only if snow conditions are favorable and avalanche danger is at a minimum. You may need crampons, ice ax, and helmet. Most climbers stay to the left of the face. At the top, a short hike on the ridge above Steel Cliffs takes you to the summit, but it is not skiable. Attempt this only if you are properly equipped and skilled.

The descent is a long, continuous run. Head down the steep Wy'east Face, veer left to descend into Superbowl, then continue down either drainage back to Hood River Meadows.

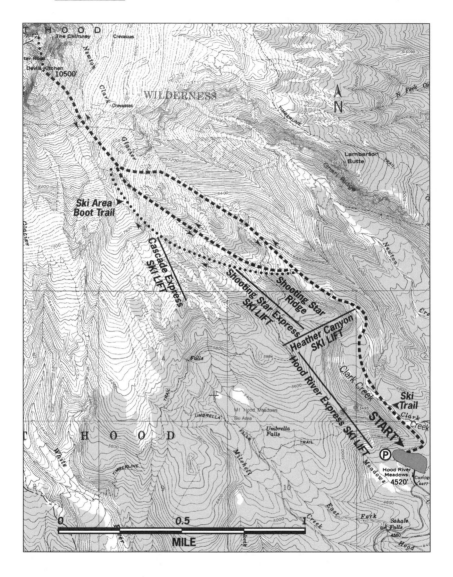

# Mount Hood North

The north side is probably the least visited and most spectacular area of Mount Hood. Year-round snow and dazzling vistas of the huge Eliot Glacier and its headwall make this trip a worthy one nearly any time of year. Not only can the snow be excellent and untracked, but the north side also has a wide variety of tours, from beginner to expert. Most of the routes are accessed from Cloud Cap Road and the Tilly Jane Historic Area.

In winter, the north side is accessed via the Tilly Jane Sno-park, near Cooper Spur Ski Area. The tours generally head through the woods to the Tilly Jane camping area and continue to Cloud Cap Saddle. You can camp in some of the buildings at Tilly Jane. An A-frame shelter is usually on a first-come first-served basis. The Tilly Jane guard station is managed by The Dalles chapter of Oregon Nordic Club. If you want to reserve a date or check availability, call the Hood River Ranger District for information. You'll also find two cookhouses, an amphitheater, and a primitive campground.

A short hike beyond Tilly Jane is Cloud Cap Saddle. In summer, a 9-mile road from the sno-park is cleared of snow and debris to allow vehicle access. Two buildings are there. Historic Cloud Cap Inn, built in 1889, is the rescue base for Crag Rats Mountain Rescue Unit. The Snowshoe Club has another building, constructed in 1910.

# Mount Hood North Maps

USFS Mount Hood Wilderness, Geo-Graphics Mount Hood Wilderness, Green Trails Mount Hood 462

# Primary Info Centers/Ranger Districts

Mount Hood National Forest Headquarters, Portland, OR: 503/668-1700; www.fs.fed.us/r6/mthood

Hood River Ranger District: 541/352-6002

# Avalanche/Weather/Road Conditions

Northwest Weather and Avalanche Center: 503/808-2400, www.nwac.noaa.gov

National Weather Service: 503/261-9246 or 360/694-6136, www.nws.noaa.gov

Oregon DOT Pass Report: 800/977-6368, www.odot.state.or.us/roads

# Ski Area Snow Reports

Cooper Spur: 503/230-2084

# Permits

Wilderness permits are required for climbing in the Mount Hood Wilderness, which includes all routes that leave Cloud Cap Saddle. Self-issued permits at no charge are available at the climbing register at the Cloud Cap campground.

A sno-park pass is required from November 15 to April 30.

A Northwest Forest Pass is required for Cloud Cap trailheads and Elk Cove.

# Of Special Note

Call ahead to check if Cloud Cap Road is open for routes starting from Cloud Cap Saddle.

# 22 Tilly Jane Trail

❄❄

| | |
|---|---|
| **Starting point** | Tilly Jane Sno-park, 3,800 feet |
| **High point** | Cloud Cap, 6,000 feet |
| **Drive distance/time** | 100 miles, 2 hours |
| **Trail distance/time** | 5 miles, 3 hours |
| **Skill level** | Beginner |
| **Best season** | Winter |
| **Maps** | USGS Mount Hood North, Geo-Graphics Mount Hood Wilderness |

Tilly Jane is a fun beginner trail akin to the south side's Alpine Trail, only steeper. It is favored by cross-country skiers and snowshoers, so it can get crowded on nice weekends in the winter. It is close to Hood River and an excellent way to get to know the north side.

Because of its low elevation, this route suffers from lousy snow. Pick this route when the snow is fast. A layer of powder over firm corn makes this a good run. Slush makes this descent slow, and snowboarders may be walking back down the lower trail.

Mount Hood's rarely visited north side

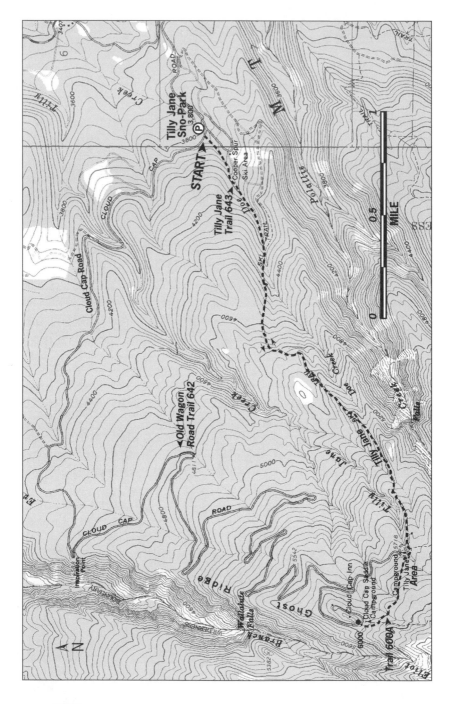

## Getting There

From Portland, drive east on Interstate 84 about 60 miles to Hood River. Head south at exit 64 on Oregon 35. Along the way, you will pass the ranger station in the town of Mount Hood. After 23 miles, turn west (right) on Cooper Spur Road. After 2 miles, turn left on Forest Road 3512, Cloud Cap Road. Continue toward Cooper Spur Ski Area and the end of the plowed road, Tilly Jane Sno-park.

## The Route

Tilly Jane Ski Trail 643 starts just up and across the road from the sno-park. Head south as the trail climbs through thick woods. In a half mile, the trail meets up with another from Cooper Spur Ski Area and continues up the hill to the right. Follow a wide path in the woods up to a ridge where you get a view to the southeast. The trail then widens and continues along the ridge west about 2 miles to the Tilly Jane area. At the Tilly Jane area you first reach the A-frame shelter, then an old cookhouse on the left. A hundred yards farther you pass an amphitheater, then cross a bridge over a small drainage. Then, on the left, is the American Legion Camp with another cookhouse, the Tilly Jane guard station, and the campground.

From the campground, continue west from Tilly Jane on Trail 600A. It winds through the woods another half mile to Cloud Cap Saddle Campground. From the campground, head a few hundred feet up the road to the Cloud Cap Inn and Snowshoe Club hut.

The descent follows the same trail. From Cloud Cap to Tilly Jane, the trail is slow. Then it steepens as it heads back down the ridge. Traverses and flat spots, especially along the last third of the descent, can make this slow, and even more so if the snow is slushy. For the lower segment, snowboarders may want to convert their splitboard to skis, put on snowshoes, or at least use poles to help coast through flat spots.

# 23 Old Wagon Road Trail

❄❄

| | |
|---|---|
| Starting point | Tilly Jane Sno-park, 3,800 feet |
| High point | Cloud Cap Saddle, 6,000 feet |
| Drive distance/time | 100 miles, 2 hours |
| Trail distance/time | 9 miles, 5 hours |
| Skill level | Beginner |
| Best season | Winter |
| Maps | USGS Mount Hood North, Geo-Graphics Mount Hood Wilderness |

Old Wagon Road is another easy trail on the north side. The historic route was first cut in 1889 and cleared for skiers in 1989. Although the ski trail is steeper than Tilly Jane, the approach is mostly flat. Like Tilly Jane, it is best descended with a layer of powder over a firm base.

## Getting There

From Portland, drive east on Interstate 84 about 60 miles to Hood River. Head south at exit 64 on Oregon 35. Along the way, you will pass the ranger

Tilly Jane Cabin, Mount Hood

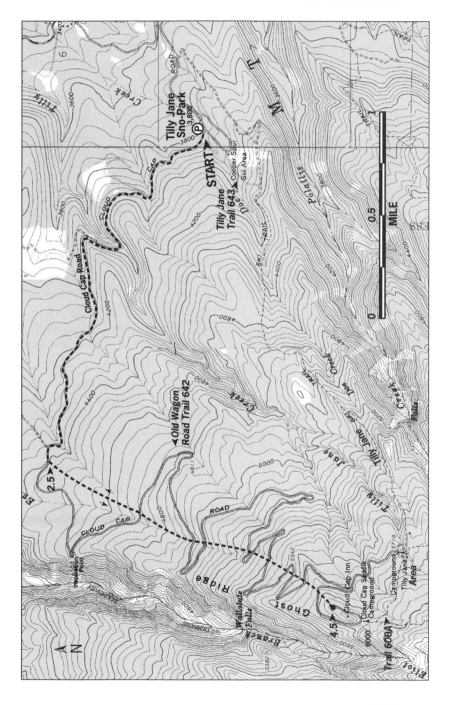

station in the town of Mount Hood. After about 23 miles, turn west (right) on Cooper Spur Road. After about 2 miles, turn left on Forest Road 3512, Cloud Cap Road. Continue toward Cooper Spur Ski Area and the end of the plowed road, Tilly Jane Sno-park.

## The Route

Ski or hike west on Cloud Cap Road, beyond the Tilly Jane Sno-park and the end of the plowed sections. The trail will likely be well-traveled. Watch for snow-mobilers on the road. Follow the road 2.5 miles to the trailhead on the left.

Head up Old Wagon Road Trail 642. The narrow trail climbs 1,500 feet directly up to Cloud Cap through thick woods. Make sure you stay to one side or the other and watch for skiers on descent. At several places the trail crosses Cloud Cap Road and should be easy to find on either side with blue-diamond trail markers. Use caution crossing the road; a steep drainage ditch on either side may be only partly filled with snow, and snowmobilers use this road. Near the top, the trail steepens, then ends at the Cloud Cap Inn and Snowshoe Club hut.

The descent heads down the trail. Keep your turns tight as it gets narrow in places. Watch for debris under the snow, especially during light-snow years.

Keep a lookout for the trail's end on Cloud Cap Road. It should be marked with a sign. You can miss the turn back to Tilly Jane Sno-park and your car. (If you do, you will keep going down to Weygandt Basin.) Once on Cloud Cap Road, it is a fairly slow ski back to the sno-park. Snowboarders will probably need to convert their splitboards back to ski mode or put on snowshoes.

## 24 MOUNT HOOD NORTH
# Cooper Spur

❄❄❄❄

| | |
|---|---|
| Starting point | Cloud Cap Saddle, 6,000 feet |
| High point | Tie-in Rock, 8,000 feet |
| Drive distance/time | 100 miles, 2 hours |
| Trail distance/time | 4 miles, 7 hours |
| Skill level | Intermediate |
| Best season | Summer |
| Maps | USGS Mount Hood North, Geo-Graphics Mount Hood Wilderness |

Cooper Spur is a large snowfield with great snow and weather in summer and fall. When the road is open, this can be a great day trip or easy overnight for those just venturing into multiday trips. Most skiers and snowboarders ascend to about 8,000 feet and ride the snowfield back to the Timberline Trail. Climbing to the summit above 8,000 feet is both technical and dangerous.

## Getting There
From Portland, drive east on Interstate 84 about 60 miles to Hood River. Head south at exit 64 on Oregon 35. Along the way, you will pass the ranger

Hiking volcanic lava above Cloud Cap, Cooper Spur to left, Mount Hood

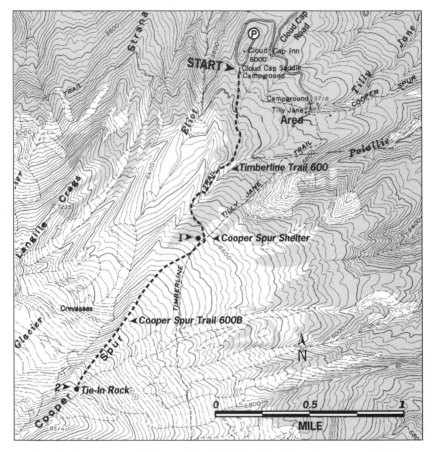

station in the town of Mount Hood. After 23 miles, turn west (right) on Cooper Spur Road. After 2 miles, turn left onto Forest Road 3512, Cloud Cap Road. Continue past Cooper Spur Ski Area and follow this steep and winding gravel road for 10 miles to Cloud Cap Saddle and the parking lot. FR 3512 is closed just past the ski area in winter and spring and usually opens around Memorial Day. The trailhead is just below and north of the Cloud Cap Inn and Snowshoe Club hut.

## The Route

Hike Timberline Trail 600 south from Cloud Cap for about 1 mile. Near a rock shelter (Cooper Spur Shelter) at about 6,640 feet, leave the Timberline Trail and take the climber's trail, 600B. Climb north up to the main ridge of

Cooper Spur, the east moraine of the huge Eliot Glacier. This lower section of the climber's trail is marked with posts.

The ridge then opens up to the large snowfield. Several fingers of gentle grade spread out across the spur. The steeper sections lie between 7,000 and 9,000 feet. The top of the recommended rideable section is at Tie-in Rock, about 8,000 feet.

The descent from Tie-in Rock can follow any of many fingers of the snowfield. The snow may be so good you can do laps. However, stay on the west section as much as possible so you minimize your hike back to the trail. The fall line will take you away from the trail, toward Cooper Spur Ski Area and the densely wooded Tilly Jane area. To find the return trail to Cloud Cap, watch for the wood posts and the small rock shelter that mark the alpine trail. Consider marking your trail with wands and use caution in poor weather.

# 25 Snowdome

❄❄❄❄❄

| | |
|---|---|
| Starting point | Cloud Cap Saddle, 6,000 feet |
| High point | Snowdome, 9,000 feet |
| Drive distance/time | 100 miles, 2 hours |
| Trail distance/time | 5 miles, 5 hours |
| Skill level | Advanced |
| Best season | Summer |
| Maps | USGS Mount Hood North, Geo-Graphics Mount Hood Wilderness |

Snowdome is a sister route to Cooper Spur, located west across the large Eliot Glacier and perhaps one of the best descents on Mount Hood, all things considered. Like Cooper Spur, it gets north sun and can be slushy in the afternoon but firms up when the sun dogs behind the west ridge. Good snow is often found here, especially late summer into fall. Snowdome is an excellent overnight trip.

Skinning up Snowdome, Mount Hood

## Getting There

From Portland, drive east on Interstate 84 about 60 miles to Hood River. Head south at exit 64 on Oregon 35. Along the way, you will pass the ranger station in the town of Mount Hood. After 23 miles, turn west (right) on Cooper Spur Road. After 2 miles, turn left onto Forest Road 3512, Cloud Cap Road. Continue past Cooper Spur Ski Area and follow this steep and winding gravel road for 10 miles to Cloud Cap Saddle and the parking lot.

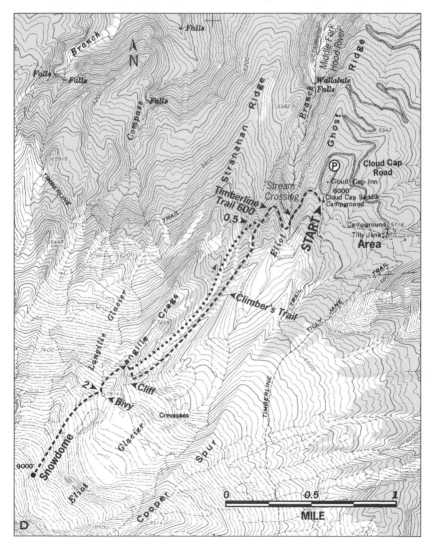

FR 3512 is closed just past the ski area in winter and spring and usually opens around Memorial Day. The trailhead is just below and north of the Cloud Cap Inn and Snowshoe Club hut.

## The Route

Hike west on Timberline Trail 600 for about a half mile to reach the Eliot Branch of the Middle Fork Hood River. This raging little creek comes right from the glacier. The Forest Service maintains a bridge in summer that may be in place. If not, use caution crossing the stream: Choose a narrow spot with large dry rocks and spot your partner. If the stream is snow-covered, use extreme caution crossing snow bridges; they can easily collapse and send you into the drink.

After crossing the stream, follow switchbacks up a steep hill. At the top, just after entering the woods, take the climber's trail that branches off to the left. Follow this through a small meadow and trees to a ridge, the west moraine of Eliot Glacier. Follow the nearly knife-edge ridge for a mile to its terminus at a cliff face, the top of the Langille Crags. Using caution, climb the steep, wide slope just to the right of the cliffs. The talus may be unstable or, if snow-covered, could avalanche.

At the top of the Crags, hike a few hundred feet to the base of Snowdome. A good bivy spot exists at the base of Snowdome at about 7,750 feet. It is just to the west of a cinder cone marked as 7,814 feet on most topo maps. Hike up the Snowdome to around 8,000 feet or 9,000 feet for steeper slopes, provided you have experience with crevasse travel.

The descent is right down the Snowdome. This wide snowfield gives room for many runs and, because it is less popular than Cooper Spur, you will likely have the place to yourself. The lower section is less steep and great for intermediate riders. If you ride the last portion where it doglegs right down to Eliot Glacier, hike back up to 7,750 feet for your hike back home. If the snow is good, earn some bonus turns just below the Langille Crags on your way home. Use caution hiking back when crossing the stream if the bridge is out: You will be tired.

## MOUNT HOOD NORTH

# 26 Langille Glacier

❄❄❄❄

| | |
|---|---|
| Starting point | Cloud Cap Saddle, 6,000 feet |
| High point | Langille Glacier, 8,300 feet |
| Drive distance/time | 100 miles, 2 hours |
| Trail distance/time | 6 miles, 6 hours |
| Skill level | Advanced |
| Best season | Summer |
| Maps | USGS Mount Hood North, Geo-Graphics Mount Hood Wilderness |

Just below and to the northwest of Snowdome, Langille Glacier is another excellent uncrowded route. Since most of the snowfields are steep but crevasse-free, they make excellent runs when the snowpack is stable, such as in summer. Because most are lower than Snowdome, they can be combined with a Snowdome run for a long descent or tried when the higher elevations have hard snow or otherwise poor conditions. You can choose among several snowfields and aspects for a whole day of riding and hiking.

Carving Langille Bowls, Mount Hood

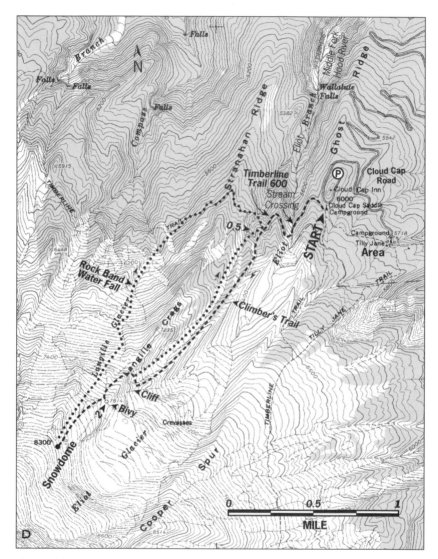

## Getting There

From Portland, drive east on Interstate 84 about 60 miles to Hood River. Head south at exit 64 on Oregon 35. Along the way, you will pass the ranger station in the town of Mount Hood. After 23 miles, turn west (right) on Cooper Spur Road. After 2 miles, turn left onto Forest Road 3512, Cloud Cap Road. Continue past Cooper Spur Ski Area and follow this steep and winding gravel road for 10 miles to Cloud Cap Saddle and the parking lot.

FR 3512 is closed just past the ski area in winter and spring and usually opens around Memorial Day. The trailhead is just below and north of the Cloud Cap Inn and Snowshoe Club hut.

## The Route

Hike west on Timberline Trail 600 for about a half mile to where you reach the Eliot Branch of the Middle Fork Hood River. This raging little creek comes right from the glacier. The Forest Service maintains a bridge in summer that may be in place. If not, use caution crossing the stream: Choose a narrow spot with large dry rocks and spot your partner. If the stream is snow-covered, use extreme caution crossing snow bridges; they can collapse easily and send you into the drink.

After crossing the stream, follow switchbacks up a steep hill. At the top, just after entering the woods, take the climber's trail that branches off to the left. Follow this through a small meadow and trees to a ridge, the west moraine of Eliot Glacier. Follow the nearly knife-edge ridge for a mile to its terminus at a cliff face, the top of the Langille Crags. Using caution, climb the steep, wide slope just to the right of the cliffs. The talus may be unstable or, if snow-covered, could avalanche.

At the top of the Crags, you have reached the bottom of Snowdome and the east edge of the Langille Glacier. A good bivy spot exists at the base of Snowdome at about 7,750 feet just to the west of a cinder cone marked as 7,814 feet on most topo maps. To reach the upper part of the Langille Glacier, head up the snowfield to the west of Snowdome and the cinder cone to 8,300 feet.

From the top of the Langille Glacier, ride the long bowl that extends down to 7,600 feet. Carefully cross a small band of rock at the bottom. At the other side, you will be at the top of the largest of Langille's bowls, the main glacier. This alone will give you an entire day of turns. At the bottom of this bowl, watch for small pools collecting runoff. For even more turns, cross yet another rock band at about 7,200 feet and ride the drainage down to the Timberline Trail if snow permits.

If it's late summer or early fall, the snow will not be sufficient to ride the lowest bowl. From the bottom of the main glacier, hike back up to the Langille Crags at 7,400 feet for your trip back down the way you came in. If the snow is good, earn some bonus turns just below the Langille Crags. Also, use caution hiking home when crossing the stream if the bridge is out: You will be tired.

## 27 | MOUNT HOOD NORTH
# Barrett Spur

✳✳✳

| | |
|---|---|
| Starting point | Elk Cove Trail, 4,400 feet |
| High point | Barrett Spur summit, 7,600 feet |
| Drive distance/time | 100 miles, 2 hours |
| Trail distance/time | 8 miles, 6 hours |
| Skill level | Advanced |
| Best season | Spring |
| Maps | USGS Mount Hood North, Geo-Graphics Mount Hood Wilderness |

Barrett Spur is one of the more remote places on Mount Hood. On the Northwest flank, the roads are not plowed to the trailhead, so access in winter and spring can be difficult. Timing in late spring or early summer is critical. The best time is when the roads and trails are clear but there is still snow above 6,000 feet. However, the snow conditions may not be great at this time of year. If you make this a one-day trip, the summer sun may turn the snow to slush. For two-day trips, Snowdome will give more riding pleasure. Nonetheless, if you want to explore this part of the mountain, Barrett Spur is a good place to start.

## Getting There

From Portland, drive east on Interstate 84 about 60 miles to Hood River. Head south at exit 64 on Oregon 35. After 13 miles, you come to the community of Mount Hood. Turn west (right) on the Hood River Highway at the Mount Hood Store. The ranger station is a half mile north on Oregon 35, so you will need to backtrack to the turnoff if you visit it. Follow the Hood River Highway about 2 miles and go right on Baseline Drive. After another mile go left on Clear Creek Road. Continue north as Clear Creek Road becomes FR 2840. Follow it to Forest Road 630. Head north 3 miles to the trailhead at the road's terminus.

## The Route

Follow Elk Cove Trail 631 and climb gently north about 3 miles through the woods to Elk Cove, a campground at the junction of the Elk Cove Trail and the Timberline Trail. At timberline, take Timberline Trail 600 west for a few

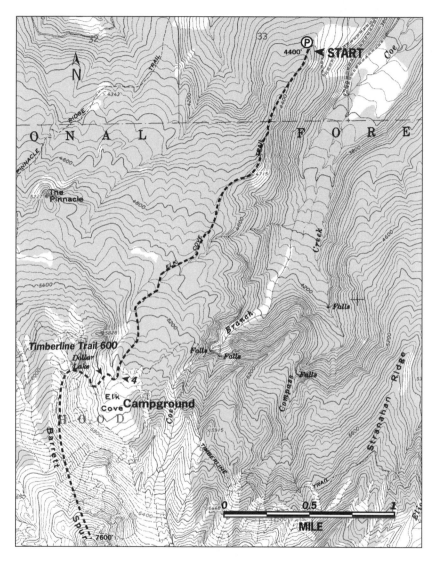

minutes until you find a spot to climb up the ridge to Barrett Spur. Once on the spur, continue due south up the wide snowfield to the summit.

The route down retraces the route up, turning on the steeper pitches off the summit, then down east-facing slopes to Elk Cove. You will have to hike back out the approach trail unless it is snow-covered and free from blowdown.

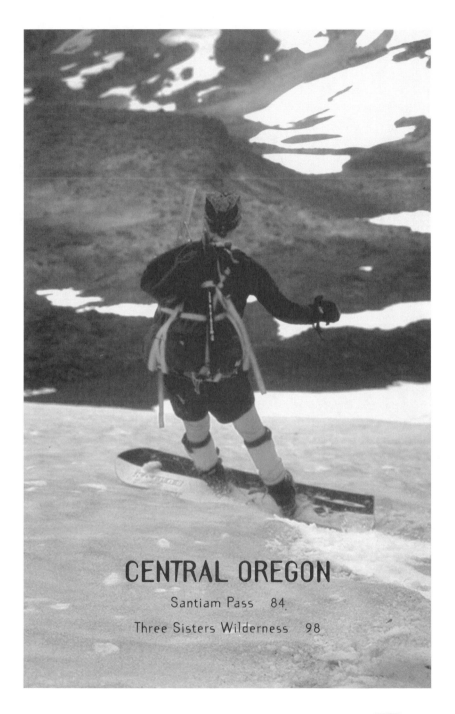

# CENTRAL OREGON

# Santiam Pass

Santiam Pass, located in the Willamette National Forest, is a frequent destination for Eugene and Salem glisse mountaineers. It offers a wide variety of routes, from cross-country trails to some of the more challenging mountaineering ascents in this book. Plan well for these routes: By the time some of the approach roads open, you may only have a short window for good snow.

Mount Jefferson is one of the more rugged and remote Cascade volcanos. It has neither the winter resorts of the Hood and Bend areas nor the numerous trails and vehicle-access lakes. However, it is one of the most spectacular areas in Oregon. Second in height only to Mount Hood, Jefferson rises 10,497 feet. The first ascent was completed in 1888 by Ray Farmer and E. C. Cross. Although many had climbed to the base of the 500-foot summit pinnacle, they were the first to reach the top.

Unlike many of the volcanos in this book, Jefferson can't be skied or snowboarded from the summit because of the pinnacle of loose volcanic rock, ice, snow, and numerous crevasses. The highest an expert can reasonably ski or snowboard from is around 9,000 feet. Jefferson Park makes a beautiful camp in the summer. In fact, it may be crowded with backpackers and mountaineers.

In comparison, Mount Washington, at 7,794 feet, is rather short in approach and descent. It makes a great spring or early summer descent for those on a time budget who can't make the two-day Jefferson trip. Like Jefferson, Washington can't be skied or snowboarded from the top. The rocky summit pinnacle takes up the top 500 feet or so. The mountain was likely named in 1871 as Washingtons Peak by a survey crew. The first ascent was

probably by a Bend group in 1923, including Ervin McNeal, Phil Philbrook, Armin Furrer, Wilbur Watkins, Leo Harryman, and Ronald Seller.

Access to the routes described here is from roads that are snow-covered in winter. Call ahead to make sure snow is melted off the road, usually after Memorial Day. The alternative is to plan for an extra day to hike the road, which makes a long trip.

## Santiam Pass Maps

USFS Willamette National Forest, Geo-Graphics Mount Jefferson Wilderness, Geo Graphics Mount Washington Wilderness

## Primary Info Centers/Ranger Districts

Willamette National Forest Headquarters, Eugene, OR: 541/465-6521, www.fs.fed.us/r6/willamette

Detroit Ranger District: 503/854-3366

McKenzie Ranger District: 541/822-3381

## Avalanche/Weather/Road Conditions

Northwest Weather and Avalanche Center: 503/808-2400, www.nwac.noaa.gov

National Weather Service: 503/261-9246, www.nws.noaa.gov

Oregon DOT Pass Report: 800/977-6368, www.odot.state.or.us/roads

## Ski Area Snow Reports

Hoodoo: 541/822-3337, hoodoo@hoodoo.com

## Permits

Wilderness permits are required for climbing in the Mount Jefferson and Mount Washington Wildernesses. Self-issued permits at no charge are available at a climbing register at the trailhead.

A Northwest Forest Pass is required for trailheads.

A sno-park pass is required for these routes between November 15 and April 30.

## Of Special Note

Call ahead to make sure the road is open to the Mount Jefferson or Mount Washington trailheads.

# 28 Mount Jefferson/ Jefferson Park Glacier

❄❄❄❄❄

| | |
|---|---|
| Starting point | Whitewater Creek Trailhead, 4,100 feet |
| High point | Jefferson Park Glacier, 8,500 feet |
| Drive distance/time | 160 miles, 3 hours |
| Trail distance/time | 14 miles, 10 hours |
| Skill level | Advanced |
| Best season | Summer |
| Maps | USGS Mount Jefferson, Geo-Graphics Mount Jefferson Wilderness |

This is one of the most scenic routes in this book. Don't set your sights on the summit unless you are an expert mountaineer; the headwall, knife-edge ridge, and summit pinnacle require technical glacier and rock climbing. Go in summer when the snow is melted from the approach trail and the Jefferson Park area. Because of the long approach and the long, steady climb up the glacier, this is best done as an overnight trip. One can sleep at the trailhead

Summer turns on Jefferson Park Glacier, Mount Jefferson

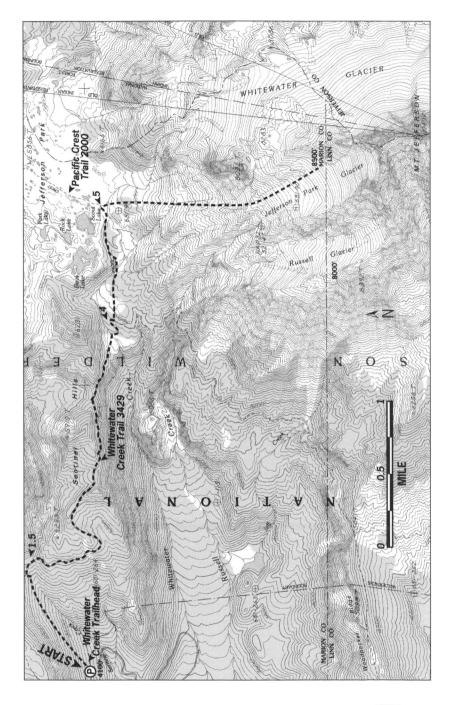

and make it halfway up the snowfield and back in a day. However, the descent will likely be in afternoon slush and you will miss the beauty of camping at Jefferson Park.

## Getting There

From Portland drive south on Interstate 5 toward Salem. At Salem, exit on Oregon 22 and head east. About 6 miles after the small town of Idanha, turn left on Whitewater Road, also called Forest Road 2243. Follow FR 2243 about 8 miles to its terminus at the Whitewater Creek trailhead.

## The Route

Follow Whitewater Creek Trail 3429. In 4 miles the trail crosses Whitewater Creek and in another half mile the trail joins Pacific Crest Trail 2000. From this junction, follow the Pacific Crest Trail north about a mile to the Jefferson Park area. Find a campsite here if making an overnight trip. If the mosquitoes or crowds are thick, climb up the snow or moraine to the south; this will give you a head start in the morning.

The climber's trail heads due south from Jefferson Park. Head directly up the snowfields below the glacier and the east moraine. After about a mile, you will reach the glacier, near 7,500 feet. Use caution and watch for crevasses. If you are inexperienced in glacier travel, head down from here. If the snow is good you can make several runs on the lower snowfields without venturing on the glacier. If you continue, stay on the climber's left, near the east moraine, to avoid crevasses. Head down from around 8,500 feet.

The descent goes directly down the way you came up. Watch for crevasses if you hiked high on the glacier. From Jefferson Park, plan to hike back out to the parking area.

# 29 Mount Jefferson/ Russell Glacier

❄

| | |
|---|---|
| Starting point | Whitewater Creek Trailhead, 4,100 feet |
| High point | Russell Glacier, 8,000 feet |
| Drive distance/time | 160 miles, 3 hours |
| Trail distance/time | 12 miles, 10 hours |
| Skill level | Advanced |
| Best season | Summer |
| Maps | USGS Mount Jefferson, Geo-Graphics Mount Jefferson Wilderness |

If you have more time and are looking for another ride on Jefferson, Russell Glacier is an option. The approach is a bit shorter but also a bit more difficult. This is still an overnight trip or a long day. In fact, plan two long days, so you can ride the Jefferson Park snowfield that evening and Russell Glacier the next day. The lower drainage of Russell Glacier does lose snow sooner in the spring than Jefferson Park, so this route is best done early in the season. Watch

Ready for a hot shower, Mount Jefferson

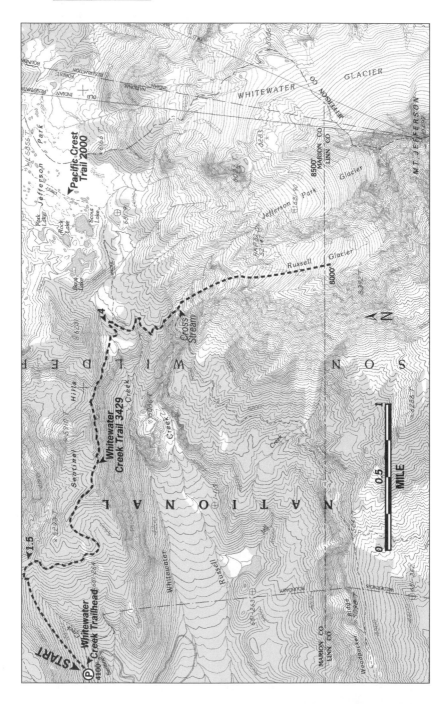

for crevasses up high. You can gain the summit ridge from here, too, and make the traverse over to the pinnacle. However, this makes a super-long trip and involves technical ice and rock climbing.

## Getting There

From Portland drive south on Interstate 5 toward Salem. At Salem, exit on Oregon 22 and head east. About 6 miles after Idanha, turn left on Whitewater Road, also called Forest Road 2243. Follow FR 2243 about 8 miles to its terminus at the Whitewater Creek trailhead.

## The Route

Follow Whitewater Creek Trail 3429 for 4.0 miles east to where it crosses Whitewater Creek. In another half mile, head south on Pacific Crest Trail 2000. After another half mile, cross the headwaters of Russell Creek. This is a hazardous crossing when the runoff is high. Use caution and spot your partners on the crossing. Then take the climber's trail southeast up the lower snowfields of Russell Glacier. Stay on the west moraine as the drainage here is steep and narrow. Those without crevasse rescue and glacier travel skills should stay on the lower snowfields, below 7,500 feet. Hike and ride several times in lieu of climbing higher on the glacier with the crevasses. Otherwise continue up toward 7,500 feet or so.

The descent goes directly down the way you came up. Watch for crevasses if you hiked high on the glacier. Also, be careful of getting low in the drainage as there is a waterfall and a narrow slot. Ride the west moraine the way you hiked up, but use caution; this is not a fall line descent but involves some traversing to rider's left.

## SANTIAM PASS
# 30 | Mount Jefferson Park Butte
### ❄❄❄

| | |
|---:|:---|
| Starting point | Whitewater Creek Trailhead, 4,100 feet |
| High point | Park Ridge, 7,000 feet |
| Drive distance/time | 160 miles, 3 hours |
| Trail distance/time | 14 miles, 10 hours |
| Skill level | Advanced |
| Best season | Summer |
| Maps | USGS Mount Jefferson, Geo-Graphics Mount Jefferson Wilderness |

If you are planning a Jefferson Park Glacier trip, Park Butte is a good option. Located at the north edge of the Jefferson Park area, it offers a good second route if Jefferson Park Glacier is too icy, too steep, or too difficult. The south-facing slopes usually soften more readily, especially in summer, so make this an early morning or late evening ride or combine it with a Jefferson Park Glacier trip.

Hiking up Jefferson Park Glacier, Park Butte in background

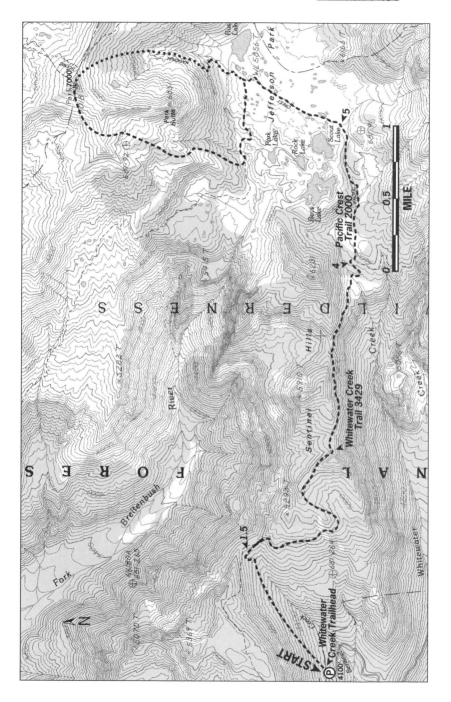

## Getting There

From Portland drive south on Interstate 5 toward Salem. At Salem, exit on Oregon 22 and head east. About 6 miles after the small town of Idanha, turn left on Whitewater Creek Road, also called Forest Road 2243. Follow FR 2243 about 8 miles to its terminus at the Whitewater Creek trailhead.

## The Route

Follow Whitewater Creek Trail 3429. In about 4 miles the trail crosses Whitewater Creek and in another half mile the trail joins Pacific Crest Trail 2000. From this junction, follow the Pacific Crest Trail north about a mile to the Jefferson Park area. Find a suitable camp here if making an overnight trip.

From Jefferson Park, Park Butte is easily identified at the north end of the lake area. Cross the meadows and climb one of the snowfields to the east or west of the butte. Continue to the top of Park Ridge at 7,000 feet.

Head down the way you came up. If you had to abort a Jefferson Park Glacier route and you have all day, yo-yo up and down the ridge. To get back to camp or the Whitewater Creek Trail, walk across the flat lake area and out the trail.

## SANTIAM PASS

# 31 Mount Washington/ Northwest Bowl

❄❄❄❄

| | |
|---|---|
| Starting point | Big Lake West, 4,680 feet |
| High point | Northwest Bowl, 7,000 feet |
| Drive distance/time | 160 miles, 3 hours |
| Trail distance/time | 10 miles, 8 hours |
| Skill level | Advanced |
| Best season | Summer |
| Maps | USGS Mount Washington, USGS Clear Lake, Geo-Graphics Mount Washington Wilderness |

Mount Washington's Northwest Bowl is a common ride for Eugene and Salem locals with only a day to spare. Drive early, start hiking by daybreak, and you can be making turns by noon. Use caution, as this route is not well-marked. Serious route finding may be needed. Mark your trail with wands if the weather is poor.

A long approach through the trees

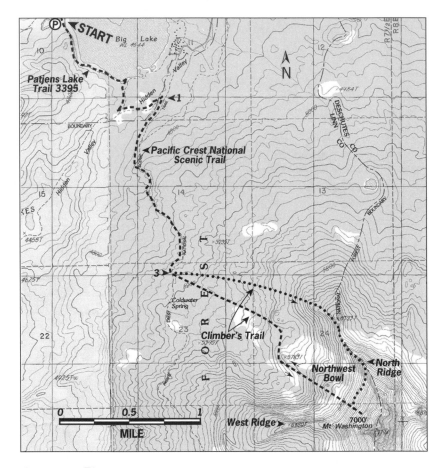

## Getting There

From Portland drive south on Interstate 5 toward Salem. At Salem, exit on
Oregon 22 and head east for 85 miles to U.S. 20/126, Santiam Junction. At
Santiam Junction, head west on Highway 20/126 for 4 miles. Turn south on
Forest Road 2690 toward Hoodoo Ski Area. Continue past the ski area about
4 miles to road's end at Big Lake West Campground.

## The Route

From Big Lake West, start around the south end of the lake on Patjens Lake
Trail 3395. After the trail leaves the lake, follow a series of trails about a mile
east to Pacific Crest Trail 2000. Hike south on the Pacific Crest Trail about a
mile to where you will find the climber's trail off to the east. When the

climber's trail splits, follow the right fork to the northwest bowl and the west ridge. (The left fork heads up to the north ridge.)

After climbing through thick woods and some meadows, you come to the bottom of the northwest bowl. Hike up the snow to about 7,000 feet, the base of the summit pinnacle.

Descend the northwest bowl to the climber's trail at timberline. Be careful you don't get off track as route finding is difficult and there are several drainages. Hike back out the approach trail.

# Three Sisters Wilderness

Three Sisters Wilderness contains some of the most unusual and tranquil scenery in Oregon. Here the Cascade volcanos meet the high desert. In summer, scents of juniper and sage mark your camp. The snow is often lighter and drier than on the west slopes of the Cascades, while the weather is more often clear and sunny, although warm days can become cold nights, even in summer. This region includes five volcanos: North Sister, Middle Sister, South Sister, Broken Top, and Mount Bachelor, although the latter is outside the wilderness area.

Access to this area is from two main towns. The high desert town of Sisters is the entry point to North Sister and Middle Sister from either the Pole Creek or Obsidian trailheads. The town of Bend and the small hub of Mount Bachelor Ski Area 20 miles west afford entry to the southern end of the wilderness.

Although it requires a long drive from Portland, South Sister is a classic ride and a good first-summit descent for intermediate riders looking for a big mountain experience. It is an annual ritual for Bend, Salem, and Eugene residents. Middle Sister's southeast ridge is one of my favorite routes in this book, a sweet ride and great overnight trip.

## Three Sisters Wilderness Maps

USFS Deschutes National Forest, Geo-Graphics Three Sisters Wilderness

## Primary Info Centers/Ranger Districts

Deschutes National Forest Headquarters, Bend, OR: 541/383-5300, www.fs.fed.us/r6/deschutes

Bend–Fort Rock: 541/383-4000

Sisters: 541/549-2111

## Avalanche/Weather/Road Conditions

Northwest Weather and Avalanche Center: 503/808-2400, www.nwac.noaa.gov

National Weather Service: 503/261-9246, www.nws.noaa.gov

Oregon DOT Pass Report: 800/977-6368, www.odot.state.or.us/roads

## Ski Area Snow Reports

Mount Bachelor, 541/382-7888, www.mtbachelor.com

## Permits

Wilderness permits are required for climbing in the Three Sisters Wilderness. Self issued permits at no charge are available at most trailheads.

A Northwest Forest Pass required for most trailheads in the Three Sisters Wilderness.

A sno-park pass is required for these routes between November 15 and April 30.

## Of Special Note

Call ahead to check road access to trailheads; some are not plowed in winter.

# 32 Middle Sister/Southeast Ridge

❄❄❄❄❄

| | |
|---|---|
| Starting point | Pole Creek Spring, 5,520 feet |
| High point | Middle Sister Summit, 10,047 feet |
| Drive distance/time | 160 miles, 3 hours |
| Trail distance/time | 14 miles, 8 hours |
| Skill level | Intermediate |
| Best season | Spring, summer |
| Maps | USGS Trout Creek, USGS North Sister, Geo-Graphics Three Sisters Wilderness |

The southeast ridge is one of the best descents in this book and an excellent nontechnical route for an overnight trip. The approach is quite long but well worth the ride if the snow is good. The 3,000-foot ride is right down the fall line. It follows a snowfield that is free of crevasses, plus the scenery is beautiful and Camp Lake is a wonderful spot to sleep out.

## Getting There

From Portland drive south on Interstate 5 toward Salem. At Salem, exit on Oregon 22 and head east to Santiam Junction where the road continues as U.S. 20 to Sisters.

Evening turns on Middle Sister

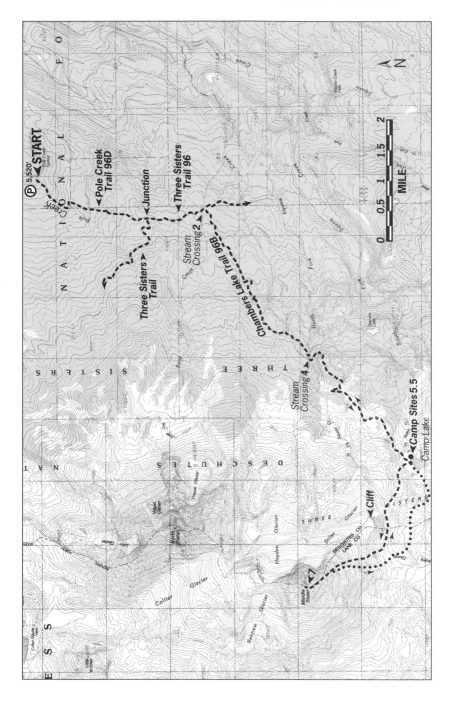

From the town of Sisters, head west on Oregon 242. After 1 mile turn south on Forest Road 15, Pole Creek Road. Follow FR 15 about 10 miles to where it dead-ends at Pole Creek Spring.

## The Route

From Pole Creek Spring follow Pole Creek Trail 96D south about 1.5 miles to the junction with Three Sisters Trail 96. Continue south on Trail 96 about another 0.5 mile to Soap Creek. Just after the trail crosses Soap Creek leave Trail 96 and take Chambers Lake Trail 96B west. You will cross a small drainage, then the North Fork Squaw Creek at 4 miles. After you reach timberline, continue on to Camp Lake, another mile and a half. At Camp Lake find a good campsite in the trees.

From Camp Lake, climb north above the lake, then head to the west of the small cliff band to gain the southeast ridge. The route follows the snowfield or the rocky ridge to about 9,000 feet, then it follows a rocky ridge of talus and scree to the summit. The last few hundred feet to the summit are rock and thus not ridable.

The descent follows the snowfields adjacent to the rocky ridge climbing route, starting at around 9,800 feet. Ride down Irving Glacier close to the bottom. You will have to traverse back to the east side of the cliffs you skirted around on the way up to ride the last 800 feet to Camp Lake. If you ride too far down Irving Glacier, you will be hiking back up the ridge to Camp Lake.

# 33 Middle Sister/Hayden Glacier

| | |
|---|---|
| Starting point | Pole Creek Spring, 5,520 feet |
| High point | Middle Sister summit, 10,047 feet |
| Drive distance/time | 160 miles, 3 hours |
| Trail distance/time | 10 miles, 8 hours |
| Skill level | Advanced |
| Best season | Summer |
| Maps | USGS Trout Creek, USGS North Sister, Geo-Graphics Three Sisters Wilderness |

A shorter but more difficult route than southeast ridge, the north face via Hayden Glacier is for experts. Simply put, you need to ascend and descend on the crevassed glacier. You will need crampons, ice ax, and full glacier travel gear. However, if you are looking for a more technical route and one that is a bit shorter, consider this trip.

## Getting There

From Portland drive south on Interstate 5 toward Salem. At Salem, exit on Oregon 22 and head east to Santiam Junction where the road continues as U.S. 20 to Sisters.

Fording North Fork Squaw Creek, Three Sisters Wilderness

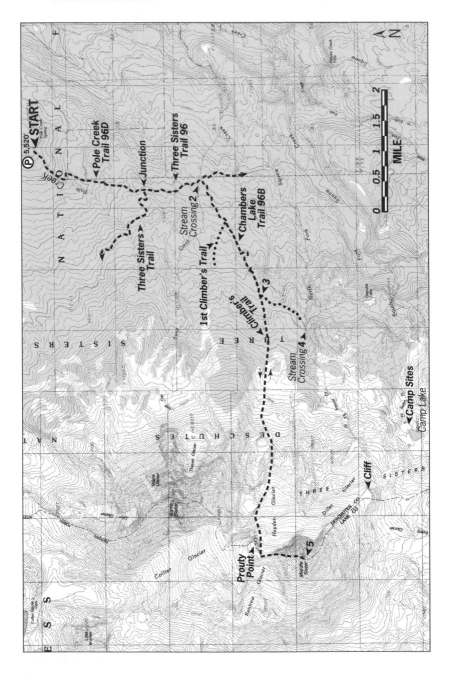

From the town of Sisters, head west on Oregon 242. After 1 mile turn south on Forest Road 15, Pole Creek Road. Follow FR 15 about 10 miles to where it dead-ends at Pole Creek Spring.

## The Route

From Pole Creek Spring follow Pole Creek Trail 96D south about 1.5 miles to the junction with Three Sisters Trail 96. Continue south on Trail 96 about another 0.5 mile to Soap Creek. Just after the trail crosses Soap Creek, leave Trail 96 and take Chambers Lake Trail 96B west toward Camp Lake. After a mile, hike past the primitive climber's trail that heads due west to North Sister. In another half mile, take the second climber's trail. If you hike past the trail, you will hit North Fork Squaw Creek in a half mile.

Follow the climber's trail west to timberline, the lower snowfields of Hayden Glacier, and the prominent rock between North Sister and Middle Sister, Prouty Point. Rope up at the glacier and stay to the right. Head for the saddle just south of Prouty Point. There are many crevasses here, so consider staying on the lower snowfield between the glacier and timberline. From Prouty Point, head due south up the north ridge to the summit of Middle Sister. There is a steep 200-foot section that may be difficult if the snow is hard or slushy, and the last few hundred feet will likely be talus.

The descent follows the north-face snowfield down to Prouty Point. Depending on snow conditions, you may need to hike down the steep section. From the saddle, cross Hayden Glacier while roped and on foot unless the crevasses are well-covered. Head back out the way you hiked in.

## THREE SISTERS WILDERNESS

# 34 | Middle Sister/Collier Glacier

| | |
|---|---|
| **Starting point** | Obsidian trailhead, 4,749 feet |
| **High point** | Middle Sister Summit, 10,047 feet |
| **Drive distance/time** | 160 miles, 3 hours |
| **Trail distance/time** | 16 miles, 10 hours |
| **Skill level** | Advanced |
| **Best season** | Summer |
| **Maps** | USGS Trout Creek, USGS North Sister, Geo-Graphics Three Sisters Wilderness |

Taking a break on the summit of Middle Sister, South Sister in background

This approach from the west to Middle Sister and North Sister is best left until the other routes in this area have been done. The long two-day ascent on the Obsidian Trail, including some glacier travel, does not have the long continuous descent of the southeast ridge. However, if you have done Middle Sister from Pole Creek and have a few days, this is a challenging climb and descent. Part of the route travels on the Collier Glacier, so you should be an expert ski and snowboard mountaineer for this route and have well-refined glacier travel skills. You will need crampons, ice ax, and full glacier travel gear. Also, the roads will be closed due to snow in the winter, so call ahead to make sure they are clear to the trailhead.

## Getting There

From Portland drive south on Interstate 5 toward Salem. At Salem, exit on Oregon 22 and head east to Santiam Junction, where the road continues as U.S. 20 to Sisters.

From the town of Sisters, head west on Oregon 242, McKenzie Pass Highway. After 17 miles, park at the Obsidian trailhead.

## The Route

Head southeast on Obsidian Trail 3528 for about 4 miles to Pacific Crest Trail 2000. This junction has a springs and waterfalls. It may be crowded in summer. Continue east on the mountaineering trail that heads toward the ridge between Renfrew Glacier and Collier Glacier. Head up the snowfield to the south arm of Collier Glacier at about 8,500 feet.

Cross Collier Glacier using extreme caution for crevasses. Head southwest on the edge of the glacier toward the small saddle just south of eminent Prouty Point at 9,312 feet. If you head east across the glacier, you will end up at the col between North Sister and Middle Sister at 8,840 feet. From here you can ride some of the slopes flanking North Sister, but you will have to traverse south to get to Middle Sister.

From Prouty Point, head due south up the north ridge to the summit. A steep 200-foot section may be difficult if the snow is hard or slushy, and the last few hundred feet will likely be talus.

The descent follows the north-face snowfield down to Prouty Point. Depending on snow conditions, you may need to hike down the steep section. From the saddle, cross Collier Glacier while roped and on foot unless the crevasses are well-covered. Head back out the Obsidian Trail.

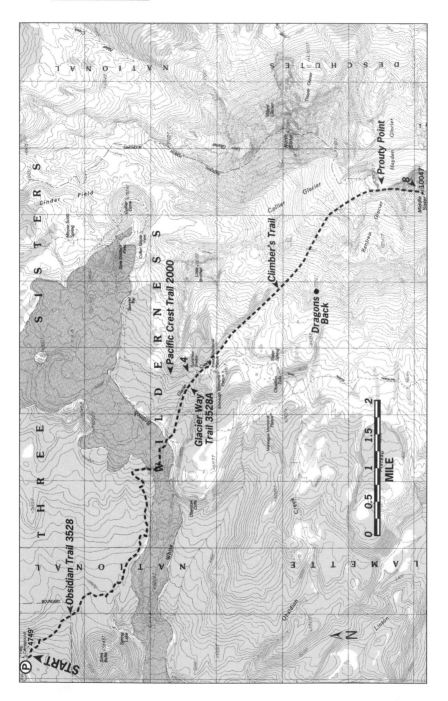

# THREE SISTERS WILDERNESS
# 35 | South Sister/Green Lakes
❄❄❄

| | |
|---|---|
| Starting point | Green Lakes trailhead, 5,450 feet |
| High point | Ridge top, 8,500 feet |
| Drive distance/time | 160 miles, 4 hours |
| Trail distance/time | 10 miles, 5 hours |
| Skill level | Intermediate |
| Best season | Spring |
| Maps | USGS South Sister, USGS Broken Top, Geo-Graphics Three Sisters Wilderness |

South Sister is one of the most accessible mountains in Oregon. The Green Lakes route gives access to the southeast side and is less crowded than the south side. Several east-facing slopes can be ridden, and the Green Lakes Trail gives good access to Broken Top, hence it is perhaps a better choice for a multiday or multimountain trip.

Above Green Lakes, South Sister in background

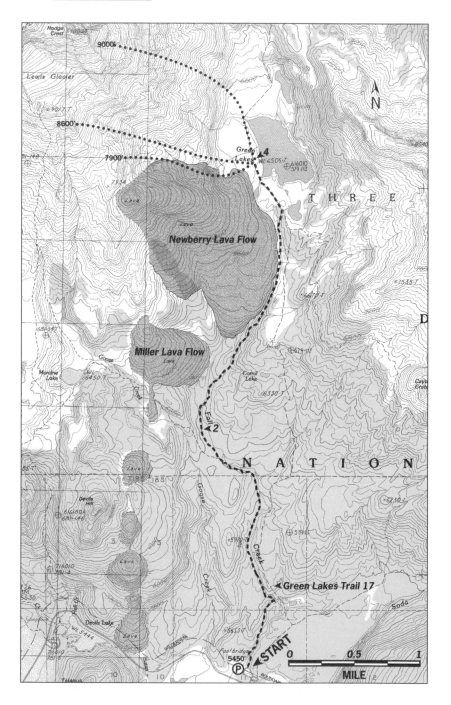

## Getting There

From Portland head east on U.S. 26 over Mount Hood and continue south to Bend following U.S. 26 then U.S. 97 from Madras. Once in Bend, follow signs to Forest Road 46, Cascade Lakes Highway, and continue west to Mount Bachelor Ski Area, about 21 miles. Continue past Mount Bachelor about 4 miles to the Green Lakes trailhead. In winter, the road ends at the ski area, so plan to ski or snowshoe the last 4 miles to the trailhead, adding an extra half day.

## The Route

Follow Green Lakes Trail 17 north along Fall Creek for 4 miles. The trail is well-traveled in summer and snow-covered in winter and early spring. The last 2 miles will be along the Miller and Newberry Lava Flows, vast expanses of rock with little vegetation. At Green Lakes, set up camp if you are staying overnight.

The best skiing and snowboarding are on any of the east-facing slopes. One route at the south end of Green Lakes follows a ridge to about 8,500 feet. A second, also the summit route described later, follows a deep drainage from the south end of the lake and up a bowl to the ridge just below Lewis Glacier. A third line follows a snowfield from the north end of the lake to the base of Hodge Crest. Take any of the three routes up to about 8,500 feet.

Descend following your climbing route. If you have time and the snow is good, you may want to ride more than one slope. If you plan an overnight trip, ride the south ridge one evening, then summit the next morning.

# 36 South Sister/ Summit via Green Lakes

❄❄❄❄❄

| | |
|---|---|
| **Starting point** | Green Lakes trailhead, 5,450 feet |
| **High point** | South Sister summit, 10,358 feet |
| **Drive distance/time** | 160 miles, 4 hours |
| **Trail distance/time** | 14 miles, 8 hours |
| **Skill level** | Advanced |
| **Best season** | Summer |
| **Maps** | USGS South Sister, USGS Broken Top, Geo-Graphics Three Sisters Wilderness |

If you have made the hike into Green Lakes and the climb to 8,500 feet, you may choose to climb another 2,000 feet to the summit of South Sister. The final climb follows a ridge that is most often without snow except for the last few hundred feet, so a summit route doesn't give you much additional vertical for turns. However, the views north to Middle Sister and North Sister and beyond are well worth the additional two hours of climbing.

Cooling off in a snow cave, Three Sisters Wilderness

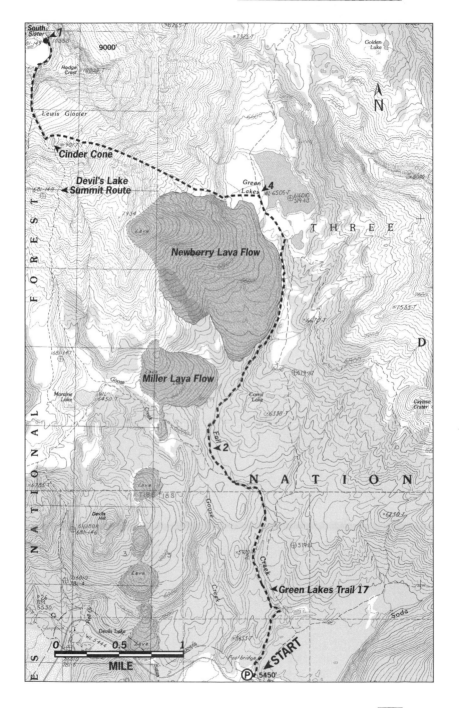

South Sister
91-143  10356

9000'

Hodge
Crest  10025-T

Lewis Glacier

Cinder Cone

Devil's Lake
Summit Route

681-149

7934

Newberry Lava Flow

Miller Lava Flow

Green
Lakes  4
WL 6505-T

616010
579 413

T H R E E

7535-T

8080-T

Golden
Lake

7325-T

8265-T

6680

N

6470-T

7535-T

629-112

Corral
Lake
6530-T

Cayuse
Crater

681-147

Goose

Moraine
Lake  WL
16450-T

Goose Creek

Creek

East

2

N A T I O N

6250-T

Devils
Hill
6380-T
681-146

Lava

519-11

5470

Goose  Creek

Creek

Green Lakes Trail 17

Soda

216010
791-4

P 26
BM
5530

Fall Cr

Devils Lake
WL 5 444  Lava

6557-T

0          0.5          1

MILE

216010
781-5

Footbridge

START

P  5450'

Lava

## Getting There

From Portland head east on U.S. 26 over Mount Hood and south to Bend following U.S. 26 and U.S. 97 from Madras. Once in Bend, follow signs to Forest Road 46, Cascade Lakes Highway, and continue west to Mount Bachelor Ski Area, about 21 miles. Continue past Mount Bachelor about 4 miles to the Green Lakes trailhead. In winter the road ends at the ski area, so plan to ski or snowshoe the last 4 miles to the trailhead, adding an extra half day.

## The Route

Follow Green Lakes Trail north along Fall Creek for 4 miles. It is well traveled in summer and snow-covered in winter and early spring. The last 2 miles will be along the Miller and Newberry Lava Flows, vast expanses of rock with little vegetation. At Green Lakes, set up camp if you are staying overnight.

The summit route follows a deep drainage from the south end of the lake, up a bowl, to the top of the snowfield. The route then winds between the Lewis Glacier and a cinder cone marked as 9,017 feet on most topo maps. Be sure to stay on one side or the other of this narrow gully to avoid avalanches, even small ones. Once through this slot, you will come to the rocky ridge that meets up with the Devils Lake Summit Route. Follow this ridge to the summit.

Descend following your climbing route. You will only be able to make turns a few hundred feet off the summit; then pack your board or skis back to the gully between the cinder cone and Lewis Glacier. Hike back down the gully to the snowfield below the ridge, or if you have glacier and crevasse experience, ride the edge of the Lewis Glacier.

You can ride all the way back to Green Lakes, then hike or ski back to the parking area.

## THREE SISTERS WILDERNESS

# 37 South Sister/Moraine Lake

❋ ❋ ❋

| | |
|---|---|
| Starting point | Devils Lake Campground, 5,450 feet |
| High point | Moraine Lake ridges, 7,000 feet |
| Drive distance/time | 160 miles, 4 hours |
| Trail distance/time | 4 miles, 3 hours |
| Skill level | Beginner |
| Best season | Spring |
| Maps | USGS South Sister, Geo-Graphics Three Sisters Wilderness |

One of the most popular routes in summer, this one can be quite peaceful in winter. Moraine Lake is very close to the road, so this makes an excellent half-day trip for Bend locals, providing the snow has melted off the road but not the moraines. Because the approach road is closed in winter, if you're willing to skin a few extra miles, you can be rewarded with great turns and solitude.

## Getting There

From Portland head east on U.S. 26 over Mount Hood. Head south to Bend following U.S. 26 then U.S. 97 heading south from Madras. Once in Bend, follow signs to Forest Road 46, Cascade Lakes Highway, and continue west to Mount Bachelor Ski Area, about 21 miles. Continue past Mount Bachelor about 6 miles to the Devils Lake trailhead. In winter the road ends at the ski area, so plan to ski or snowshoe the last 6 miles to the trailhead, adding an extra half day.

## The Route

Hike due north on Devils Lake Trail 36. The steep trail winds along the Hell Creek drainage. Be sure to stay on one side or the other of the creek and watch for small sloughs. Later in spring this trail will be free from snow, but mud and downed timber may make it just as slow going. This trail leads you between two hills, Kaleetan Butte and Devils Hill.

At about 6,700 feet you will reach the intersection with Moraine Lake Trail 17.1. Follow this east for less than a half mile to Moraine Lake, then hike any one of the moraines to the west, east, or north.

Make turns down to your heart's content. The route follows any ridge down to the lake. Traverse back to the Devils Lake Trail. With adequate snow cover and minimal downed timber and forest debris, you may be able to ski most of the way down to the parking lot.

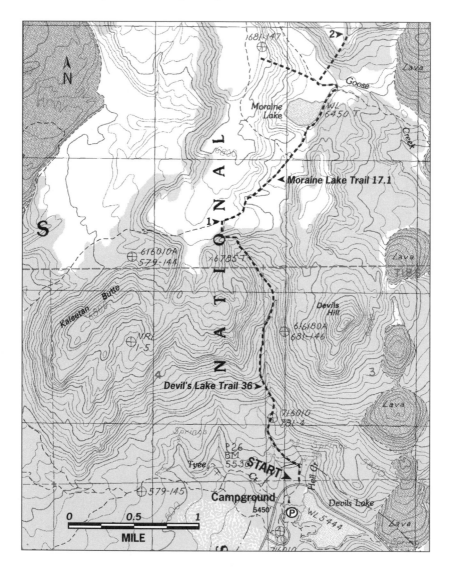

# 38

## South Sister/
## Summit via Moraine Lake

❄ ❄ ❄ ❄ ❄

| | |
|---|---|
| Starting point | Devils Lake Campground, 5,450 feet |
| High point | South Sister summit, 10,358 feet |
| Drive distance/time | 160 miles, 4 hours |
| Trail distance/time | 7 miles, 6 hours |
| Skill level | Advanced |
| Best season | Spring |
| Maps | USGS South Sister, Geo-Graphics Three Sisters Wilderness |

This is one of the most popular summer routes, perhaps because it is easy to get to, nontechnical, and beautiful. In fact, next to Mount Hood, this may well be the most popular climb in Oregon. It is accessible and the route to the summit is straightforward. Some backcountry skiers and snowboarders do this every spring as a ritual. By summer, hoards of climbers and hikers will swarm this route.

## Getting There

From Portland head east on U.S. 26 over Mount Hood. Head south to Bend following U.S. 26 and then U.S. 97 from Madras. Once in Bend, follow signs to Forest Road 46, Cascade Lakes Highway, and continue west to Mount Bachelor Ski Area, about 21 miles. Continue past Mount Bachelor about 6 miles to the Devils Lake trailhead. In winter the road ends at the ski area, so plan to ski or snowshoe the last 6 miles to the trailhead, adding an extra half day.

## The Route

Hike due north on Devils Lake Trail 36. The steep trail winds along the Hell Creek drainage. Be sure to stay on one side or the other of the creek and watch for small sloughs or avalanches. Later in spring this trail will be free from snow, but mud and downed timber may make it just as slow going. This trail leads you between two hills, Kaleetan Butte and Devils Hill. At about 6,680 feet you will pass the intersection with Moraine Lake Trail 17.1. Find a suitable campsite in this broad, flat area if you are planning a two-day trip.

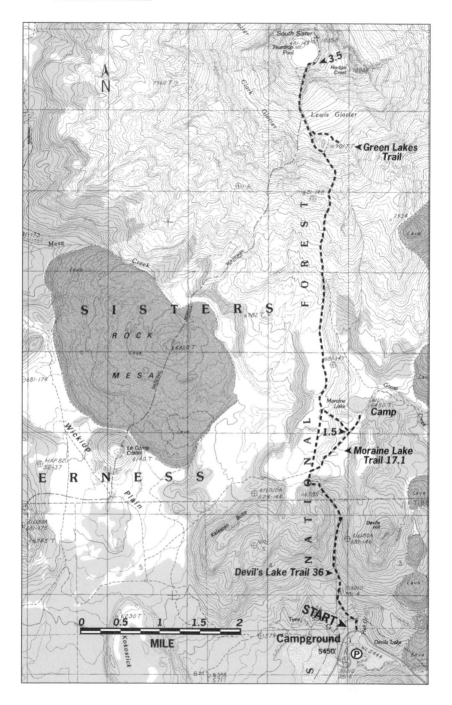

South Sister

Teardrop Pool

▲3.5

Hodge Crest

Lewis Glacier

◄Green Lakes Trail

SISTERS

ROCK MESA

FOREST

Moraine Lake

Camp

Goose

1.5

◄Moraine Lake Trail 17.1

ERNESS

Wickiup Plain

Le Conte Crater

NATIONAL

Devils Hill

Devil's Lake Trail 36►

START▲

0    0.5    1    1.5    2

MILE

Campground
5450'

Ⓟ

Continue north across the flats toward the summit, hike up the snowfield, and gain the main ridge. Once on the ridge, follow this rocky trail or the snowfields to the summit. Toward the summit at about 9,000 feet the trail meets up with the Green Lakes Trail. Stay well above and to the west of Lewis Glacier. The trail follows a windblown talus ridge to the summit, where all but the last few hundred feet are bare of snow.

The descent follows the snowfields adjacent to the ascent trail. With enough snow you should be able to connect snowfields all the way to the flats near Moraine Lake, with the occasional hike over a rock band or two. Once back on the Devils Lake Trail, with adequate snow cover and minimal downed timber and forest debris, you may be able to ski most of the way down to the parking lot.

# 39 Broken Top/Crater Bowl

❄❄❄

| | |
|---|---|
| **Starting point** | Broken Top trailhead, 7,000 feet |
| **High point** | Crater Bowl, 8,500 feet |
| **Drive distance/time** | 160 miles, 4 hours |
| **Trail distance/time** | 6 miles, 5 hours |
| **Skill level** | Advanced |
| **Best season** | Spring |
| **Maps** | USGS Broken Top, Geo-Graphics Three Sisters Wilderness |

Although the approach area is popular for cross-country skiers and snowmobilers, Broken Top is definitely an advanced trip for downhillers. In winter, you will likely need to break trail once beyond the Dutchman Flat area, and you may need to do some serious route finding in the thick woods. After the road opens in late spring or early summer, timing is critical. You will want the snow to be off the road and trail so that approach is clean, but not melted off the flanks of the mountain.

At camp at Green Lakes, Three Sisters Wilderness

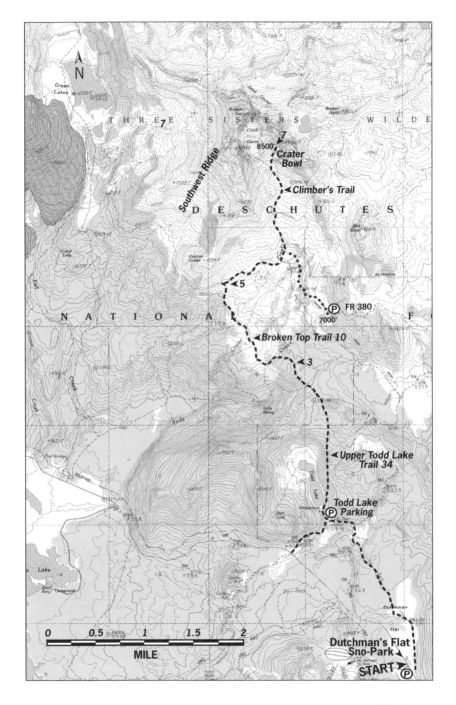

Green
Lakes

T H R E E ⊕ 7 S I S T E R S ⊕ W I L D E

Southwest Ridge

8500' ◄ 7
Crater
Bowl

◄ Climber's Trail

D E S C H U T E S

Coral
Lake

◄ 5

⊕ P FR 380
7000'

N A T I O N A L

◄ Broken Top Trail 10

◄ 3

◄ Upper Todd Lake
Trail 34

P Todd Lake
Parking

Dutchman

Dutchman's Flat
Sno-Park

START ► P

| 0 | 0.5 | 1 | 1.5 | 2 |

MILE

## Getting There

From Portland head east on U.S. 26 over Mount Hood. Head south to Bend following U.S. 26 and then U.S. 97 from Madras. Once in Bend, follow signs to Forest Road 46, Cascade Lakes Highway, and continue west to the Mount Bachelor Ski Area, about 21 miles. In winter, follow signs to Dutchman Flat Sno-park. In spring, you may be able to drive another half mile to Todd Lake.

In summer, continue past the ski area about 2 miles and turn right on Todd Lake Road to the Todd Lake parking area. Continue driving past Todd Lake on Three Creek Lake Road, also called Forest Road 370. After about 3.5 miles, turn left on FR 380 to the trailhead, which is the closest to FR 380. However, if the snow is melted sufficiently to get here, there may not be much of it on Crater Bowl.

## The Route

In winter or spring, start from Dutchman Flat Sno-park or Todd Lake, respectively. Go north on Upper Todd Lake Trail 34 through the woods for 2 miles and connect with Broken Top Trail 10, heading northeast. After a mile, head north on a climber's trail along the Crater Creek drainage to the foot of Crater Bowl.

Alternatively, from FR 380 hike Broken Top Trail 10 about 1 mile to Crater Creek drainage and the climber's trail. From here the climber's trail follows Crater Creek drainage to the base of Crater Bowl.

From the foot of the south-facing bowl at 7,000 feet, choose a line and hike to the top. Around 8,500 feet you will reach a rock band that continues west toward Crook Glacier and the rocky summit. The summit is a climbing route that requires a rope and rock-climbing protection if you want to stash your boards and get the full adventure.

Descend from 8,500 feet down one of many lines to the bottom of the bowl. Hike or skin back out the approach trail you came in on. Watch for avalanche danger, too, as this bowl is steep. In winter, slabs can release easily. In spring watch for wet point-release slides, especially in the afternoon.

# 40 | Broken Top/Southwest Ridge

❅ ❅ ❅

| | |
|---|---|
| Starting point | Green Lakes trailhead, 5,450 feet |
| High point | Broken Top, southwest ridge, 8,000 feet |
| Drive distance/time | 160 miles, 4 hours |
| Trail distance/time | 8 miles, 10 hours |
| Skill level | Advanced |
| Best season | Spring |
| Maps | USGS Broken Top, Geo-Graphics Three Sisters Wilderness |

The southwest ridge is probably one of the more popular Broken Top routes because it can be combined with a South Sister trip. Because of the fairly low elevation, it is best to go in spring or early summer before snow melts. It is accessible from the Broken Top Trail or via the Green Lakes Trail when combined with South Sister (see Routes 35 and 36).

Above Green Lakes, Broken Top in background

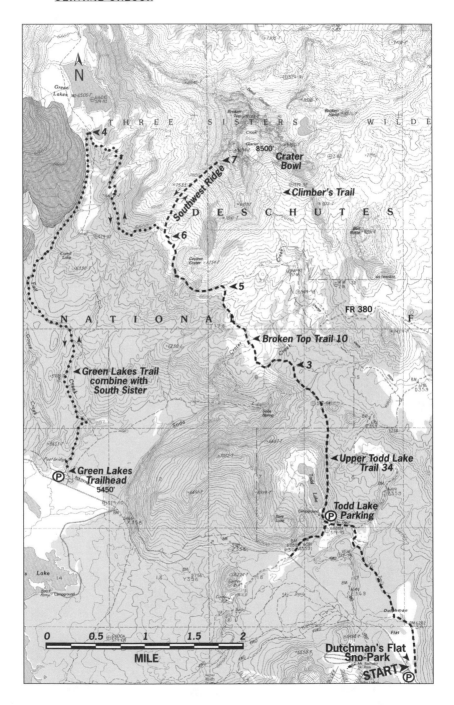

## Getting There

From Portland head east on U.S. 26 over Mount Hood. Head south to Bend following U.S. 26 and then U.S. 97 from Madras. Once in Bend, follow signs to Forest Road 46, Cascade Lakes Highway, and continue west to Mount Bachelor Ski Area, about 21 miles. In winter, start from Dutchman Flat Sno-Park. In spring, continue a half mile past Mount Bachelor to Todd Lake.

To combine a Broken Top trip with South Sister, continue past Mount Bachelor about 4 miles to the Green Lakes trailhead. Keep in mind that in winter the road ends at the ski area, so you should plan to ski or snowshoe the last 4 miles to the trailhead, adding an extra half day.

## The Route

From Dutchman Flat or Todd Lake, head north on Upper Todd Lake Trail 34. About 4 miles from Dutchman Flat head west on Broken Top Trail 10. After 2 more miles you will come to the base of the southwest ridge.

Alternatively, follow Green Lakes Trail 17 along Fall Creek north for 4 miles. It is well-traveled in summer and snow-covered in winter and early spring. Head southeast from Green Lakes on Broken Top Trail 10. Use care crossing Fall Creek, especially if on a snow bridge or downed tree. After 1.5 miles or so you will be at the foot of the southwest ridge, a long gentle slope.

Climb up to around 8,200 feet on the southwest ridge. Descend down the broad ridge. Head back out through Green Lakes or Dutchman Flat, whichever way you came in.

## THREE SISTERS WILDERNESS
# 41 Mount Bachelor/ Northeast Ridge

❄❄

| | |
|---|---|
| Starting point | Blue Lodge or Sunrise Lodge, 6,400 feet |
| High point | Mount Bachelor summit, 9,065 feet |
| Drive distance/time | 160 miles, 4 hours |
| Trail distance/time | 4 miles, 3 hours |
| Skill level | Beginner |
| Best season | Winter |
| Maps | USGS Bachelor Butte, USGS Broken Top |

Bachelor makes a great starting point for those just beginning. Although the ski area covers the entire mountain, this is still a backcountry destination. Early in the season or after the area closes in summer, there can be good snow. It is accessible year-round for an easy half-day trip from Bend. If you climb during hours of lift operation, check with the ski patrol and stay clear of runs. Several ridges lead to the top from the northeast. Be prepared for a great workout.

Evening alpenglow on Bachelor's north face

## Getting There

From Portland head east on U.S. 26 over Mount Hood. Head south to Bend following U.S. 26 and then U.S. 97 from Madras. Once in Bend, follow signs to Forest Road 46, Cascade Lakes Highway, and continue west to Mount Bachelor Ski Area, about 21 miles. Follow signs to the Blue Lodge or Sunrise Lodge parking area.

## The Route

From Blue Lodge or Sunrise Lodge, follow one of the main ridges or ski runs to timberline, at the top of the Sunrise lift. Then climb up the northeast ridge, just east of the Summit lift, to the top. At the top of the Summit lift, traverse and climb a few hundred feet west to the actual summit. The route is a steady,

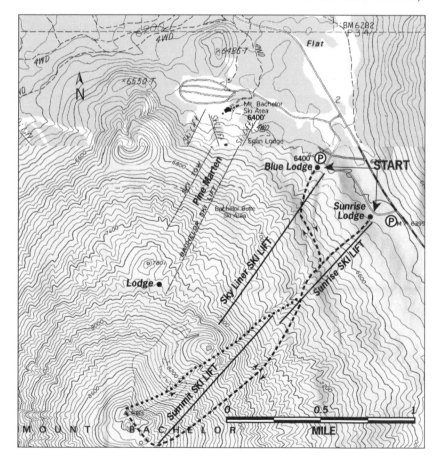

nontechnical climb that varies in steepness. Because of ski-area signs, runs, and lifts, the route is easy to follow.

The ride down follows the route up, staying on any one of the numerous glades or cleared runs of the ski area. Alternatively, ski or snowboard the steep north-facing cirque down to around 7,200 feet. Join the ascent route and head back to the parking area.

# 42

## Mount Bachelor/North Face

❄❄

| | |
|---:|:---|
| Starting point | Mount Bachelor main parking lot, 6,400 feet |
| High point | Mount Bachelor summit, 9,065 feet |
| Drive distance/time | 160 miles, 4 hours |
| Trail distance/time | 4 miles, 3 hours |
| Skill level | Beginner |
| Best season | Winter |
| Maps | USGS Bachelor Butte, USGS Broken Top |

Glacier runoff, Three Sisters Wilderness

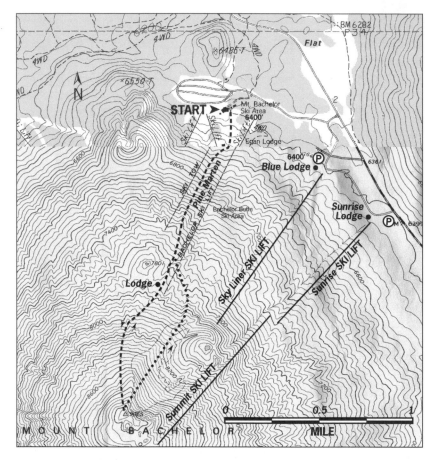

Like the northeast route, the north side of Bachelor is busy during ski season, which extends into spring and summer, but just after or before the season you may find some snow worth riding, especially if you are pressed for time or just starting out in backcountry. As always, if you climb during hours of lift operation, check with the ski patrol and stay clear of runs.

## Getting There

From Portland head east on U.S. 26 over Mount Hood. Head south to Bend following U.S. 26 and then U.S. 97 from Madras. Once in Bend, follow signs to Forest Road 46, Cascade Lakes Highway, and continue west to Mount Bachelor Ski Area, about 21 miles. Follow signs to the main lodge parking area.

## The Route

Head up one of the main ridges or broad ski runs alongside the Pine Marten lift. Above timberline, around 7,800 feet, you will pass the Pine Marten Lodge. Continue south toward the summit on a broad, low-angle ridge that is just west of the north-facing cirque.

The descent goes down the northwest ridge, or more often right down the north cirque. On the lower half of the mountain, follow any of the numerous glades or cleared runs back to the parking lot.

# SOUTHERN OREGON

# Willamette Pass

Willamette Pass is another local spot for mid–Willamette Valley residents, especially snow riders from Eugene. Like Santiam Pass, it offers a plethora of cross-country ski trails and a small ski resort. The backcountry options include Diamond Peak, a relatively obscure Cascade volcano.

Diamond Peak is fairly difficult to access. In winter, the nearest plowed road makes the north approach a super-long, super-flat skin, in which you will likely be breaking trail. After the roads clear in spring, the approach from the west is easier, but route finding is difficult as there is no established mountaineering trail on Diamond Peak.

For the best bet, go in late spring, and gather as much information about road, trail, and snow conditions as possible. Be prepared for route finding with a map, compass, altimeter, and GPS.

## Willamette Pass Maps

USFS Willamette National Forest, Imus Geographics Diamond Peak Wilderness

## Primary Info Centers/Ranger Districts

Willamette National Forest Headquarters, Eugene, OR: 541/465-6521, www.fs.fed.us/r6/willamette

Middle Fork Ranger District: 541/782-2283

## Avalanche/Weather/Road Conditions

Northwest Weather and Avalanche Center: 503/808-2400, www.nwac.noaa.gov

National Weather Service: 503/261-9246, www.nws.noaa.gov

Oregon DOT Pass Report: 800/977-6368, www.odot.state.or.us/roads

## Permits

Wilderness permits are required for the Diamond Peak Wilderness. Free, self-issued permits are available at the trailhead or ranger station.

A sno-park pass is required between November 15 and April 30.

A Northwest Forest Pass is required the rest of the year.

## Of Special Note

Call ahead to make sure the road is open to the trailhead, usually in June.

Be advised that there is no regional avalanche report. The Oregon report is generally for Northern Oregon.

# 43 | Diamond Peak/West Shoulder

❄

| | |
|---|---|
| Starting point | Corrigan Lake trailhead, 5,000 feet |
| High point | Diamond Peak summit, 8,744 feet |
| Drive distance/time | 160 miles, 3 hours |
| Trail distance/time | 6 miles, 5 hours |
| Skill level | Advanced |
| Best season | Spring |
| Maps | USGS Diamond Peak |

The west approach for Diamond Peak is fairly difficult because the trail is primitive and the wilderness remote. Route finding is difficult. Fortunately, there are fewer people here than on almost any of the other routes. If you time it right so that the road is open but there is still snow on the flanks of the mountain, this can be a great day trip. As always, plan for an unexpected night out if the weather turns poor and the route is obscured.

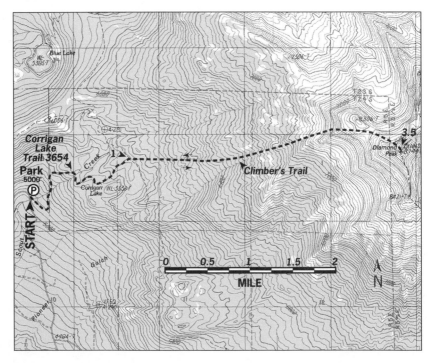

## Getting There

From Portland drive south on Interstate 5 for about 110 miles to Eugene. Just south of Eugene, head east on Oregon 58. Follow Oregon 58 about 35 miles to Oakridge. From Oakridge, take Forest Road 21 south along Hills Creek Reservoir, then east. After 30 miles, take FR 2149 another 5 miles to the Corrigan Lake trailhead.

## The Route

Hike east on Corrigan Lake Trail 3654. In a mile it intersects Trail 3699. Continue past Trail 3699 to where the Corrigan Lake Trail becomes a primitive climber's trail or nonexistent. Follow the main ridge northwest. You will be between the two branches of the Scout Creek headwaters. Hike through the woods at timberline and climb the west shoulder. A small, lower summit and saddle at 8,306 feet make a lower destination if conditions up higher are not good. Otherwise, continue up the west side to the summit.

Descend the west shoulder back to timberline. Be careful that you don't ride the southwest bowl, as this will take you far from the trail back to Corrigan Lake. Depending on snow conditions, hike or ski back out.

# Diamond Lake

The Diamond Lake area routes can be the easiest or the most difficult trips you've ever done. If you try them in winter and poor weather, you may have difficult route finding, tough high camps, and long approaches. In spring, after snow has melted from the approach trails, climbing to these peaks, all under 10,000 feet, can be relatively straightforward. Winter can get busy here with snowmobiles; late spring offers the most peaceful days with good weather.

There is another option on Mount Bailey: It is the only Oregon area that has a snowcat operation with no developed ski resort. There are a number of important points to bear in mind. First, Mount Bailey Snowcats operates December to April, so you may hear the roar of the cat on the southeast ridge and have your fresh tracks snaked by snowcat skiers and snowboarders. Second, if you are a novice and looking for a backcountry experience, Mount Bailey Snowcats has experienced guides to help you explore the wild Southern Oregon snow. Third, avalanche danger is a paramount concern. Mount Bailey Snowcats does some avalanche control. Also, a group of snowcat clients can kick a slide down on top of you, if you are lower on the mountain. Check with Mount Bailey Snowcats prior to heading out on your own in winter or early spring.

Mount Thielsen is not guided. Marked by a rocky summit pinnacle, it is rugged terrain and less traveled than other routes. It was first climbed by USGS survey ensign E. E. Hayden in 1883. Frequent lightning storms and the prominent summit pinnacle have prompted the moniker, "Lightning Rod of the Cascades."

Besides the snowcats, you will find a plethora of cross-country and snowmobile terrain in the Diamond Lake area, so the place is busy. Diamond Lake Resort offers lodging for those driving from afar looking for a cushy trip.

## Diamond Lake Maps

USFS Umpqua National Forest; USFS Rogue-Umpqua Divide, Boulder Creek, and Mount Thielsen Wildernesses

## Primary Info Centers/Ranger Districts

Umpqua National Forest Headquarters: www.fs.fed.us/r6/umpqua
Diamond Lake Ranger District: 541/498-2531

## Avalanche/Weather/Road Conditions

Northwest Weather and Avalanche Center: 503/808-2400,
www.nwac.noaa.gov

National Weather Service: 503/261-9246, www.nws.noaa.gov

Oregon DOT Pass Report: 800/977-6368, www.odot.state.or.us/roads

## Permits

Wilderness permits are required for the Mount Thielsen Wilderness. Free,
self-issued permits are available at the trailhead.

A sno-park pass is required for these routes between November 15 and
April 30.

A Northwest Forest Pass is required for these routes the rest of the year.

## Of Special Note

Mount Bailey Snowcats operates on Mount Bailey from December to April;
contact www.mountbailey.com or 800/446-4555. For lodging or snow information, try Diamond Lake Resort, 800/733-7593.

Be advised that there is no regional avalanche report. The Oregon report is
generally for Northern Oregon.

# 44 Mount Bailey/Southeast Ridge

❄❄❄❄❄

| | |
|---|---|
| Starting point | Mount Bailey trailhead, 5,300 feet |
| High point | Mount Bailey summit, 8,368 feet |
| Drive distance/time | 270 miles, 4 hours |
| Trail distance/time | 12 miles, 10 hours |
| Skill level | Advanced |
| Best season | Spring |
| Maps | USGS Diamond Lake, USGS Pumice Desert West |

Mount Bailey offers a plethora of turns, especially if you go with Mount Bailey Snowcats. If you plan a winter trip, you will need two days for the long approach. The best option for hiking is late spring or early summer when you can drive to the trailhead and the snowcat operation will be closed. There will still be plenty of snow up high and you can do the route in a day.

## Getting There

From Portland drive south on Interstate 5 for about 185 miles to Roseburg. Head east on Oregon 138, North Umpqua Highway. After 80 miles you come to the east shore of Diamond Lake and the town of the same name. Continue to the south side of the lake, and head west on Oregon 230. In winter, you can drive less than half a mile to the sno-park. In summer, continue a few hundred yards and turn north on Forest Road 6542 toward the south shore camping area. After 0.5 mile, turn west on FR 4795. Drive another 2 miles and turn south on FR 300. Drive a few hundred yards to the Mount Bailey trailhead.

## The Route

Head northwest through the woods on the Mount Bailey Trail. The trail is marked for cross-country skiers and follows the southeast ridge through the woods up above timberline. Watch for snowcat skiers, especially if they are doing avalanche control. To get to the summit, hike west around the prominent hill at 7,800 feet and continue up the southwest summit pitch.

Descend the south bowl and southeast ridge. Ski out the trail. Snowboarders may need poles to push themselves along the ski track in the flats.

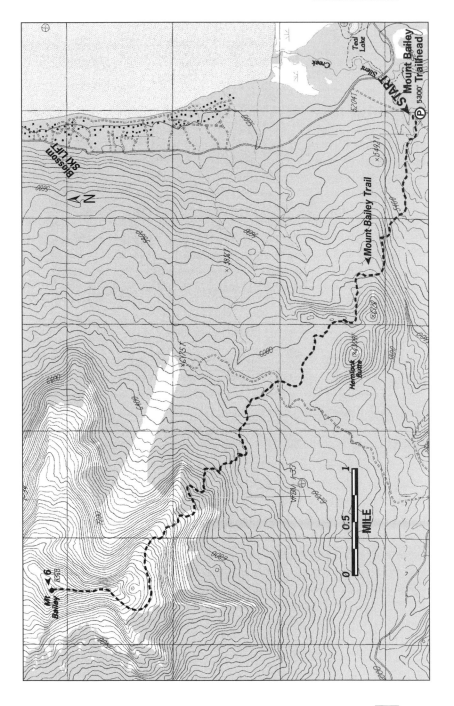

# 45

## Mount Thielsen/West Face

| | |
|---|---|
| **Starting point** | Mount Thielsen Sno-park, 5,300 feet |
| **High point** | Mount Thielsen West Face, 8,500 feet |
| **Drive distance/time** | 265 miles, 4 hours |
| **Trail distance/time** | 9 miles, 10 hours |
| **Skill level** | Intermediate |
| **Best season** | Spring |
| **Maps** | USGS Diamond Lake, USGS Mount Thielsen |

If you have time, consider adding Mount Thielsen to your Mount Bailey trip. The turns are not as steep, but the approach is fairly straightforward and you can add another peak to your list. You can't ride off the summit though, a rocky pinnacle that requires rock climbing skill and equipment.

## Getting There

From Portland drive south on Interstate 5 for about 185 miles to Roseburg. Head east on Oregon 138, North Umpqua Highway. After about 80 miles you'll come to the east shore of Diamond Lake and the town of the same name. Continue to the south side of the lake. About 3 miles past the Diamond Lake Resort access road is the sno-park.

## The Route

Head east up Mount Thielsen Trail 1456, which is marked with the blue diamonds of cross-country ski trails. After a long mile, it passes Spruce Ridge Trail and follows up steeper slopes. After 2 more miles, the trail passes Pacific Crest Trail 2000. Once at timberline, follow the west ridge climber's trail. The slopes between 6,000 and 8,000 feet are best for skiing. You may have to search for clean lines or hike well above timberline. Watch for boulders and light snow cover.

Descend to timberline and hike or ski out the approach trail.

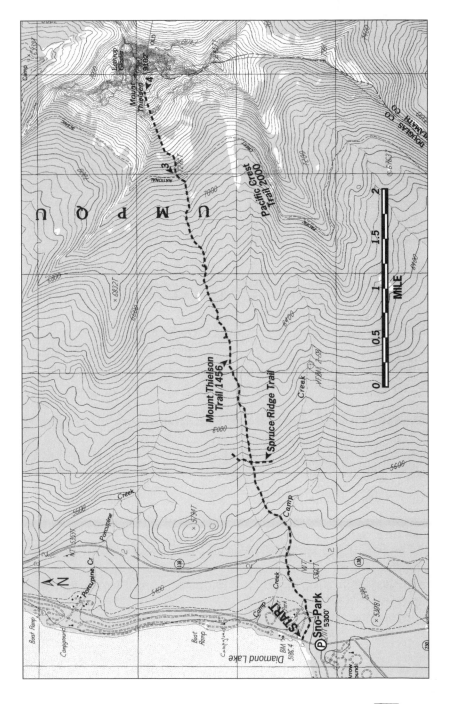

# Winema Wilderness

The Winema Wilderness is the backyard for Klamath Falls residents. If you make the trip down from the Willamette Valley, pay close attention to conditions. You don't want to make the long drive for lousy snow. In spring, good corn and nice weather can make the turns worth the long drive.

Two highlights worth noting are found here. Mount McLoughlin is a large volcano within the Sky Lakes Wilderness, and Pelican Butte is a cinder cone that offers access to snow in winter and spring. Both have gentle slopes and steeps. Because of their location, snow can be wildly variable. There may be light, dry powder or heavy Cascade crud. Before you make the journey down, follow conditions for several weeks. Make sure you have both good snow and good weather in the forecast.

## Winema Wilderness Maps

USFS Winema National Forest, USFS Sky Lakes Wilderness

## Primary Info Centers/Ranger Districts

Winema National Forest Headquarters: 541/883-6714, www.fs.fed.us/r6/winema

Klamath Ranger District: 541/885-3400

## Avalanche/Weather/Road Conditions

Northwest Weather and Avalanche Center: 503/808-2400, www.nwac.noaa.gov

National Weather Service: 503/261-9246, www.nws.noaa.gov

Oregon DOT Pass Report: 800/977-6368, www.odot.state.or.us/roads

## Permits

Wilderness permits are required for the Sky Lakes Wilderness. Free, self-issued permits are available at the trailhead.

A sno-park pass is required for these routes between November 15 and April 30.

A Northwest Forest Pass is required for Mount McLoughlin.

# Of Special Note

A Pelican Butte ski area (www.pelican2000.com) in Winema National Forest may be a reality in the near future.

There is no regional avalanche report. The Oregon report is generally for Northern Oregon.

Call ahead to check road conditions.

# 46

## WINEMA WILDERNESS
## Mount McLoughlin/ Southeast Ridge

❄❄❄❄❄

| | |
|---|---|
| **Starting point** | Mount McLoughlin trailhead, 5,600 feet |
| **High point** | Mount McLoughlin summit, 9,495 feet |
| **Drive distance/time** | 325 miles, 6 hours |
| **Trail distance/time** | 11 miles, 10 hours |
| **Skill level** | Intermediate |
| **Best season** | Spring |
| **Maps** | USGS Mount McLoughlin |

This is a great trip, located in the Sky Lakes Wilderness, for southern Oregon locals who live in Medford or Klamath Falls, especially those looking for a big mountain climb and descent. For those living elsewhere, it can be combined with an extended trip to the Diamond Lake area, but it is worth a long drive

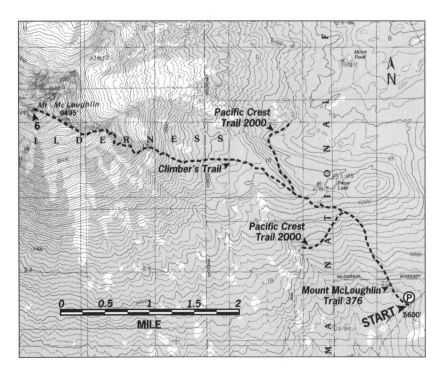

on its own. The challenging but nontechnical climb is marked by numerous lakes, rocky ground, and thick trees. Good weather makes this a great trip; poor weather and snow make the drive a waste of time. Plan carefully.

## Getting There

Head south on Interstate 5 for about 283 miles to Medford. Head north on Oregon 62 for 6 miles, then east on Oregon 140, Lake of the Woods Highway. In 32 miles turn north on Four Mile Lake Road, Forest Road 3650. After 2 miles, turn left on FR 3361. Look for the trailhead in a quarter mile.

## The Route

Take Mount McLoughlin Trail 3716 heading northwest. The trail winds through woods and among large rocks. After a mile from the parking lot it joins the Pacific Crest Trail 2000 for a quarter mile. The climber's trail branches off the Pacific Crest Trail and continues up steeper slopes. At timberline, it reaches the southeast ridge and follows the ridge to the summit. The last 1,000 feet are on an open ridge.

To descend, ski down the southeast ridge. If you ride the bowls to the east or south, watch the ridgeline for descent. Don't get skewed to one side or the other or you'll need to hike back to the trail at timberline.

# 47 Pelican Butte

❄ ❄ ❄

| | |
|---|---|
| Starting point | Cold Spring trailhead, 5,800 feet |
| High point | Pelican Butte summit, 8,036 feet |
| Drive distance/time | 340 miles, 5 hours |
| Trail distance/time | 6 miles, 5 hours |
| Skill level | Advanced |
| Best season | Winter |
| Maps | USGS Pelican Butte, USGS Crystal Spring |

Pelican Butte is a local hot spot for Klamath Falls skiers and snowboarders. Just north of Klamath Lake, the low elevation suffers from marginal snow but offers easy access. For Northern or Central Oregon residents, combine this with a Mount McLoughlin trip if the snow is good or the weather and avalanche risk make McLoughlin too difficult. In spring, timing is everything. You will want the snow melted enough so you can drive to the Cold Spring

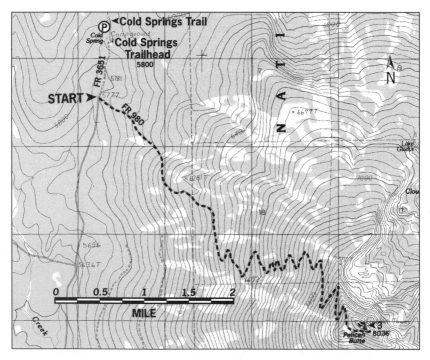

Campground, but with enough left on the upper slopes to ride. Be advised: There are snowmobiles on this route.

## Getting There

Head south on Interstate 5 for about 283 miles to Medford. Head north on Oregon 62 for 6 miles, then east on Oregon 140, Lake of the Woods Highway. In 45 miles, take Forest Road 3651 north where it branches from Oregon 140. Follow this road about 8 miles north toward Cold Spring Campground. The summit road, FR. 980, is a quarter mile south of the trailhead on the right. Depending on snow coverage, you may not be able to drive all the way to the trailhead.

There are several alternatives. One is to drive another mile on Oregon 140 and turn north on Westside Road at Upper Klamath Lake. Then drive north for about 5 miles to the east side of Pelican Butte. Take FR 230 on the left and park at the gate.

Another option is to access the butte from the south. From Oregon 140, head north on Westside Road and take a left on FR 3455. The road ends on the south face of Pelican Butte.

## The Route

From the west side, follow FR 980 to the summit. The initial road is a low grade through forest. It then climbs 2,000 feet on a series of switchbacks. The summit is an old lookout.

From the summit, ride down the road or use the summit as a base to ride the northwest or southwest bowls. Hike back to the summit for the ride down the road, though, to get back to your vehicle without getting lost.

# NORTHEAST OREGON

# Eagle Cap Wilderness

The Eagle Cap Wilderness and surrounding area are remote, uncrowded, and beautiful. This area is frequented by Northeast Oregon locals, and more snow gliders from the west side of the state are venturing here. It is marked by high alpine lakes, rugged peaks, and large basins. Because of the drier climate, the snow conditions can be excellent.

The hub of the Eagle Cap backcountry scene is the small town of Joseph. Here you will find lodging and restaurants. Day trips can be made from several sno-parks just south of Joseph, in particular Salt Creek Summit, McCully Basin, and South Wallowa Lake. For the most part, these are winter and early spring routes as the snow melts much faster here than on the glaciated peaks of the Cascades.

For those traveling from elsewhere, guided trips are an excellent option. Two guide services offer day tours, hut/cabin overnight trips, and avalanche seminars. If you are a beginner or intermediate, consider the multiday hut/cabin avalanche seminar. Not only will you get a multitude of turns in this area, you will drive away much more learned on avalanche safety.

## Eagle Cap Wilderness Maps
USFS Wallowa-Whitman National Forest, Imus-Geographics Eagle Cap Wilderness

## Primary Info Centers/Ranger Districts
Wallowa-Whitman National Forest Headquarters: 541/523-6391, www.fs.fed.us/r6/w-w

Eagle Cap Ranger District: 541/426-4978

## Avalanche/Weather/Road Conditions
Northwest Weather and Avalanche Center: 503/808-2400, www.nwac.noaa.gov

National Weather Service: 503/261-9246, www.nws.noaa.gov

Oregon DOT Pass Report: 800/977-6368, www.odot.state.or.us/roads

## Permits
Wilderness permits are required for the Eagle Cap Wilderness. Free, self-issued permits are available at the trailhead.

A sno-park pass is required for these routes between November 15 and April 30.

A Northwest Forest Pass is required for these routes.

## Of Special Note

Wing Ridge Ski Tours operates a number of huts and cabins: Aneroid Lake Cabins, Big Sheep Shelter, Bonny Lakes Shelter, and Wing Ridge Shelter. Check www.wingski.com or call 800/646-9050.

Be advised that there is no regional avalanche report. The Oregon report is generally for Northern Oregon.

## EAGLE CAP WILDERNESS
# Aneroid Lake

❄ ❄ ❄ ❄

| | |
|---|---|
| Starting point | Wallowa Lake trailhead, 4,670 feet |
| High point | Tenderfoot Pass, 8,500 feet |
| Drive distance/time | 325 miles, 5 hours |
| Trail distance/time | 16 miles, 8 hours |
| Skill level | Advanced |
| Best season | Winter |
| Maps | USGS Joseph, USGS Aneroid Mountain |

This route is guided by Wing Ridge Ski Tours and is offered some years as an avalanche course. The steady climb to base camp at Aneroid Lake Cabins gives access to several days of skiing and snowboarding the basin and flanks of Aneroid Mountain. Because it has such a long approach, it is best done as an overnight tour.

## Getting There

Head east on Interstate 84 about 260 miles to La Grande. Head north on Oregon 82 and follow signs to Enterprise. At Enterprise head south to Joseph. About 7 miles south of Joseph, Highway 82 ends at the Wallowa Lake Sno-park and trailhead.

## The Route
From Wallowa Lake Sno-park, the route follows Trail 1804 up the East Fork Wallowa River. The trail follows switchbacks through the forest and past a dam and into the Eagle Cap Wilderness. The trail continues through meadows and up to Aneroid Lake Shelter about 7 miles from the trailhead. From the cabins, the large Aneroid basin on the flanks of Aneroid Mountain can be hiked and skied. Use caution for avalanches here. For more options, skin to Tenderfoot Pass or Dollar Lake Pass.

The descent follows the trail back down along the East Fork Wallowa River. For snowboarders, short skis or splitboards are recommended, especially with parties of skiers. The rolling hills are not necessarily conducive to snowshoes, and with skis or splitboards you can trade tracks with skiers.

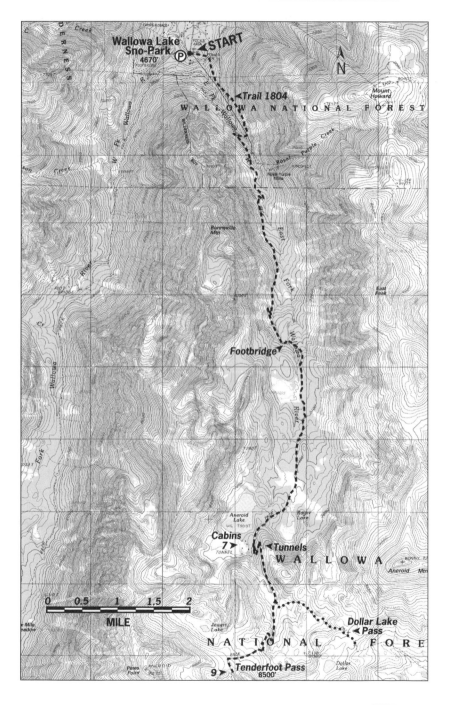

# 49

## EAGLE CAP WILDERNESS
# Wing Ridge

❄❄❄❄❄

| | |
|---|---|
| **Starting point** | Salt Creek Summit Sno-park, 6,120 feet |
| **High point** | Wing Ridge Shelter, 7,220 feet |
| **Drive distance/time** | 340 miles, 5 hours |
| **Trail distance/time** | 4 miles, 3 hours |
| **Skill level** | Intermediate |
| **Best season** | Winter |
| **Maps** | USGS Aneroid Mountain, USGS Lick Creek |

This route is a short, popular trip that can be crowded on weekends. Wing Ridge Ski Tours guides here and in some years offers an avalanche course. From Salt Creek Summit Sno-park, one can access the steep slopes of Wing Ridge fairly quickly.

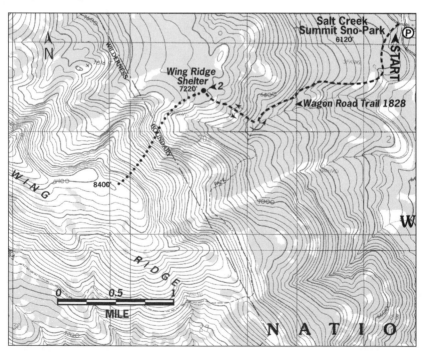

## Getting There

Head east on Interstate 84 about 260 miles to La Grande. Head north on Oregon 82, following signs to Enterprise. At Enterprise head south to Joseph. From Joseph, continue southeast on County Road 350 about 8 miles. Turn right on Forest Road 39. In 10 miles, Salt Creek Summit Sno-park is at the end of the plowed road.

## The Route

The route follows Wagon Road Trail 1828 south, and after a mile or so it branches west up the short, steep pitch to the Wing Ridge Shelter. From the shelter, one can continue up the steeper slopes of Wing Ridge, where it tops out at 8,800 feet.

Ski or snowboard the east-facing slopes of Wing Ridge, paying close attention to avalanche danger. Then ride down the slopes you skinned up on from the shelter. Watch for people coming up the trail. There are several lines, so spread out and yo-yo.

# 50 McCully Basin

| | |
|---|---|
| **Starting point** | McCully Basin Sno-park, 5,520 feet |
| **High point** | Wing Ridge, 8,700 feet |
| **Drive distance/time** | 325 miles, 5 hours |
| **Trail distance/time** | 14 miles, 12 hours |
| **Skill level** | Intermediate |
| **Best season** | Winter |
| **Maps** | USGS Joseph, USGS Kinny Lake, USGS Aneroid Mountain |

McCully Basin is a third Wallowa trip that is also guided. The approach offers some low-angle turns. It is a popular cross-country ski trail, and it may be best for cross-country skiers or downhillers who plan a multiday trip with the guide service. The upper basin has many steep shots—a week's worth if you have the time. Like Aneroid Basin, McCully Basin is almost too far for a one-day trip.

## Getting There

Head east on Interstate 84 about 260 miles to La Grande. Head north on Oregon 82, following signs to Enterprise. At Enterprise head south to Joseph. From Joseph, continue southeast on County Road 350 about 5 miles. Turn right on County Road 633, Tucker Downs Road, which continues as Forest Road 3920. About a mile past the Ferguson Ridge Ski Area, the road ends at McCully Basin Sno-park.

## The Route

From the sno-park, follow McCully Creek Trail 1812. It follows an old road through the woods and then along McCully Creek for several miles to McCully Basin. At timberline, around 7,600 feet, the basin opens up. The McCully Huts are here. You can continue south up to the saddle on Wing Ridge. Other options include hiking and riding the west basin flanks. Numerous routes on the west side of the basin go up to around 8,000 feet.

The descent follows the long, slow McCully Creek Trail. Snowboarders will want short skis or a splitboard, as snowshoes make travel very slow on this trail.

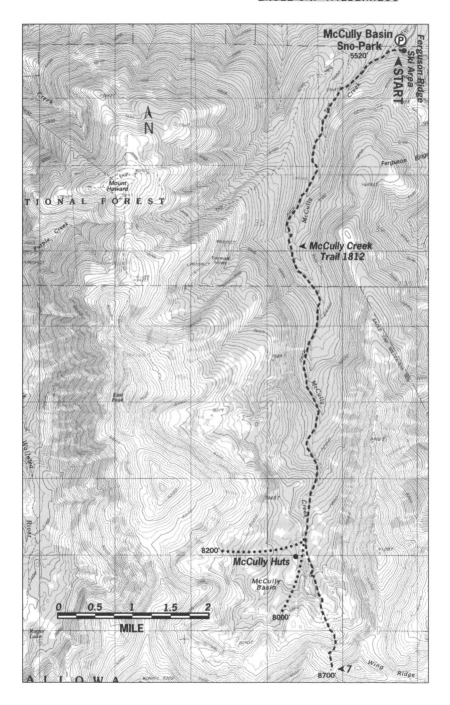

# SOUTHWEST WASHINGTON

# Mount Adams

At 12,276 feet, Mount Adams is the second highest peak in Washington. Much of it lies in the Mount Adams Wilderness; the east flank is part of the Yakama Indian Reservation. The Klickitat and Yakama tribes call this peak Pahto, "son of the Great Spirit." It was given its current name, after President John Adams, by Thomas Farnham in 1843, when the Cascades were known as the President's Range.

The first ascent was reported in 1854 by A. G. Aiken, Edward J. Allen, and Andrew Burge, and since then the south-side summit has seen lots of climbing activity. In the 1920s a lookout tower was stationed on the summit, and in the 1930s a sulfur mine operated out of a shack that is still visible in late summer. The first descent on skis was in 1932 by a group led by University of California ski coach Walter Mosauer.

The backcountry skiing here is endless. The foothills are popular for snowshoers and Nordic skiers. The south side is the hub of skiing and climbing in late spring and throughout the summer.

## Mount Adams Maps

USFS Gifford Pinchot National Forest, USFS Mount Adams Wilderness, USFS Mount Adams Ranger District

## Primary Info Centers/Ranger Districts

Gifford Pinchot National Forest Headquarters, Vancouver, WA: 360/891-5000, 24-hour recording at 360/891-5009, climbing recording at 360/891-5015, www.fs.fed.us/gpnf

Mount Adams Ranger District: 509/395-2501

## Avalanche/Weather/Road Conditions

Northwest Weather and Avalanche Center: 503/808-2400, www.nwac.noaa.gov

National Weather Service: 503/261-9246 or 360/694-6136, www.nws.noaa.gov

Washington DOT Pass Report: 888/766-4636, www.wsdot.wa.gov/sno-info

## Permits

Self-issued wilderness permits are available at a box outside the Mount Adams Ranger Station with 24/7 access. A climber's registration form is required at the time of permit.

The Cascade Volcano Pass was new in 1999. It is now required for climbing above 7,000 feet on Mount Adams from July 1 to October 31 for every person in your group. For a weekend trip, a $15 pass is good for Friday through Sunday. For a weekday trip, a $10 pass is valid for a Monday through Thursday trip. An annual Cascade Volcano Pass for $30 is good for multiple trips to Mount Adams and Mount St. Helens. Permits are available at the Mount Adams Ranger Station.

A sno-park permit is required from October 1 to May 1 for designated lots.

All the routes starting at Cold Springs require a Northwest Forest Pass. However, the Cascade Volcano Pass includes a parking voucher.

## Of Special Note

Call ahead to check if the road from Morrison Creek to Cold Springs is open. Usually it is clear after Memorial Day.

# 51

## MOUNT ADAMS
## South Climb

❄❄❄❄❄

| | |
|---|---|
| **Starting point** | Cold Springs, 5,600 feet |
| **High point** | Mount Adams summit, 12,276 feet |
| **Drive distance/time** | 120 miles, 2 hours |
| **Trail distance/time** | 10 miles, 9 hours |
| **Skill level** | Advanced |
| **Best season** | Summer |
| **Map** | USGS Mount Adams East |

The south climb is the most popular glisse and climbing route on the mountain. This classic climb is a great way to get big mountain experience when you have only a weekend to spare. However, on nice summer weekends it can get overcrowded. It is considered a nontechnical summit climb, but snow riders should still have mountaineering experience to make the ascent. On hard snow, crampons and an ice ax may be necessary.

Many climb and glide Mount Adams in two days, camping midmountain. However, it can be done as a daylong round-trip from Cold Springs with a predawn start. Fewer yet climb it in winter or spring before the road is clear. The section between Morrison Creek and Cold Springs will not be passable until late May or June, so call ahead or be prepared for a long hike to timberline.

Mount Adams, a.k.a. Pahto

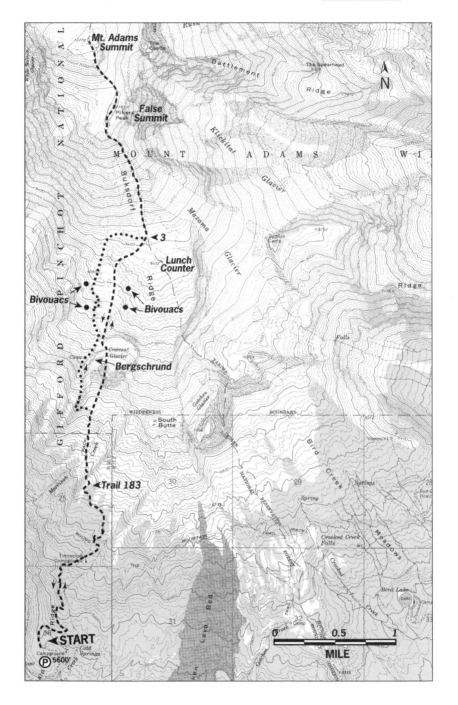

# Getting There

From Portland drive east on Interstate 84 for 60 miles to Hood River. Take exit 63 and cross north to Washington on the Hood River Toll Bridge. Over the bridge, turn left and head west on Washington 14 for 2 miles. Turn right and head north on Washington 141 for 25 miles to Trout Lake. At Trout Lake, take the left fork to the ranger station, a mile north of town on the left.

After obtaining a permit, drive back to Trout Lake and follow the other fork north. In a few miles, turn left on Forest Road 80, marked by a "South Climb" sign. After a few miles continue on FR 8040. The final section from Morrison Creek Horse Camp to Cold Springs is rough and unimproved. You should have a sturdy vehicle with high clearance, although some passenger cars can make the road when conditions are good.

# The Route

A trail register and gate mark an old road, Trail 183, which leads to the timberline camp. At timberline the trail crosses the Round-the-Mountain Trail at 6,380 feet. Continue on the climber's trail to the bottom of Crescent Glacier. Gain the top of the glacier by climbing directly up the face to the north or northeast. Alternatively, skirt the bottom of Crescent Glacier to the west and gain the rocky ridge that parallels the glacier to the west. Recently, poles have been placed to mark this route. Avoid climbing up the glacier to the northwest as a bergschrund opened in 1997 and snow bridges may not be safe.

At the top of Crescent Glacier, about 8,500 feet, you should reach the first of many rock shelters on either side of the snowfield. Continue up the snowfield to a wide flat spot at 9,400 feet, called Lunch Counter.

From Lunch Counter, the route is straight up Suksdorf Ridge to Pikers Peak, also called the "False Summit." This long, steady climb takes about two hours. It may be too steep to skin, but you may find a staircase of boot steps all the way up. At the False Summit, the true summit is visible on a clear day across the saddle and to the northwest.

The route down follows the route up. The pitch below the summit is steep. From the False Summit, ride the long and steady 35-degree pitch in one run if you have any legs left. From Lunch Counter, veer south to glide the low-angle snowfield above Crescent Glacier; stop to pick up your overnight gear if you camped. Then descend the steep bowl of Crescent Glacier. Again, watch for the bergschrund on the west side of the glacier. In spring, you can glide most of the way to timberline, then hike back to Cold Springs.

# 52 | MOUNT ADAMS
## Crescent Glacier
❄❄❄

| | |
|---|---|
| Starting point | Cold Springs, 5,600 feet |
| High point | Lunch Counter, 9,400 feet |
| Drive distance/time | 120 miles, 2 hours |
| Trail distance/time | 6 miles, 5 hours |
| Skill level | Intermediate |
| Best season | Summer |
| Map | USGS Mount Adams East |

For snow riders lacking time, skill, or experience for the summit climb, Crescent Glacier is a fun route in summer. If the snow is good, you can hike up and make several runs on the glacier bowl. The section between Morrison Creek and Cold Springs will not be passable until late May or June, so call ahead or be prepared for a long hike to timberline.

## Getting There
From Portland drive east on Interstate 84 for 60 miles to Hood River. Take exit 63 and cross north to Washington on the Hood River Toll Bridge. Over

Crossing the saddle between False Summit and the summit, Mount Adams

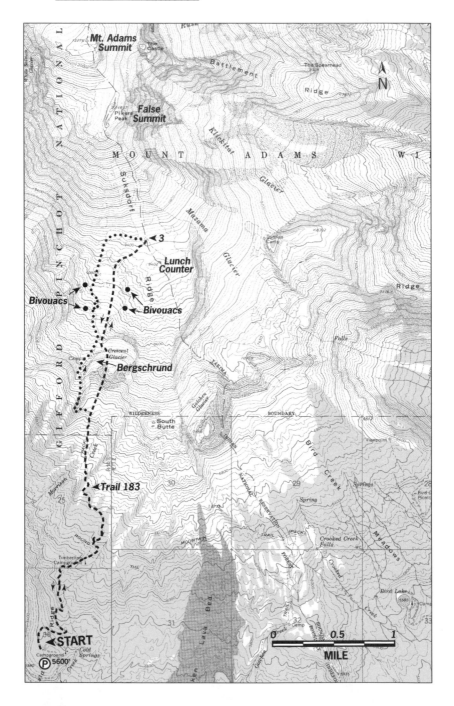

the bridge, turn left and head west on Washington 14 for 2 miles. Then turn right and head north on Washington 141 for 25 miles to Trout Lake. At Trout Lake, take the left fork to the ranger station, a mile north of town on the left.

After obtaining a permit, drive back to Trout Lake and follow the other fork north. In a few miles, turn left on Forest Road 80, marked by a "South Climb" sign. After a few miles continue on FR 8040. The final section from Morrison Creek Horse Camp to Cold Springs is rough and unimproved. You should have a sturdy vehicle with high clearance, although some passenger cars can make the road when conditions are good.

## The Route

At Cold Springs, a trail register and gate mark an old road, Trail 183, that leads to the timberline camp. At timberline the trail crosses the Round-the-Mountain Trail at 6,380 feet. Continue on a primitive climber's trail past timberline to the bottom of Crescent Glacier. Gain the top of the glacier by climbing directly up the glacier face to the north or northeast. Recently, poles have been placed marking this route. Avoid climbing up the glacier to the northwest as a bergschrund opened in 1997 and snow bridges may not be safe.

Above Crescent Glacier is a low-angle snowfield to a wide, flat bench at 9,400 feet called "Lunch Counter." This may not be worth riding, but with an extra hour and 1,000 feet of climbing, you get a better view of Suksdorf Ridge and campsites for a later summit trip.

The route down stays close to the climbing route in the bowl of Crescent Glacier. If it gets tracked up, skirt a bit to the east. Watch for the bergschrund off to the west on the way down. If conditions are good, you may want to hike back up for another run or two. The best turns will probably be between 7,000 and 8,500 feet. In spring, you can glide most of the way to timberline and then hike back to Cold Springs.

# 53 | MOUNT ADAMS
## Southwest Chute

❄❄❄❄❄

| | |
|---|---|
| Starting point | Cold Springs, 5,600 feet |
| High point | False Summit, 11,657 feet |
| Drive distance/time | 120 miles, 2 hours |
| Trail distance/time | 9 miles, 8 hours |
| Skill level | Advanced |
| Best season | Summer |
| Map | USGS Mount Adams East |

The Southwest Chute is one of the finest descents in this book. This narrow 4,000-foot gully maintains a 35-degree slope from the False Summit to timberline. Because of its steepness, timing is important. It should be ridden in early summer, early in the day. With fresh snow, ice, or slush, avalanche danger or risk of a fall can be significant. Many people ride this in a day with an early start from Cold Springs. For an overnight, consider camping at timberline. If you camp at Lunch Counter, you will need to carry your overnight gear with you on the descent or hike back up and retrieve it after you ride the chute.

Basic backcountry pack

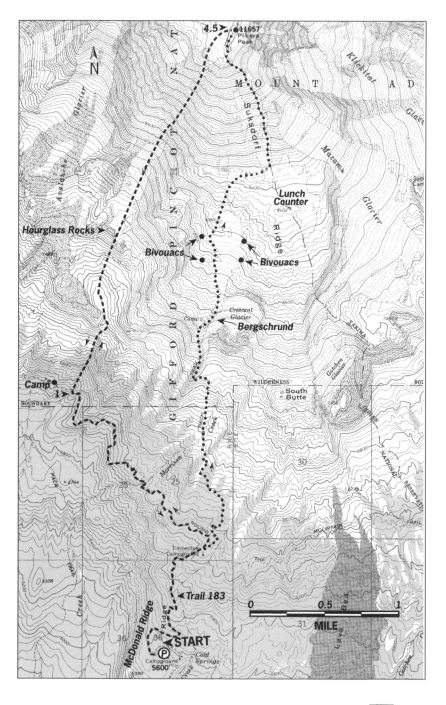

## Getting There

From Portland drive east on Interstate 84 for 60 miles to Hood River. Take exit 63 and cross north to Washington on the Hood River Toll Bridge. Turn left and head west on Washington 14 for 2 miles. Turn right and head north on Washington 141 for 25 miles to Trout Lake. At Trout Lake, take the left fork to the ranger station, a mile north of town on the left.

After obtaining a permit, drive back to Trout Lake and follow the other fork north. After a mile, turn left on Forest Road 80, marked by a "South Climb" sign. After a few miles the road becomes FR 8040 and turns to gravel. The final section from Morrison Creek Horse Camp to Cold Springs is rough and unimproved. You should have a sturdy vehicle with high clearance, although some passenger cars can make the road when conditions are good.

## The Route

At Cold Springs, a trail register and gate mark an old road, Trail 183, which leads to the timberline camp. At timberline the trail crosses the Round-the-Mountain Trail at 6,380 feet. Head west on the Round-the-Mountain Trail over McDonald Ridge. After about a mile, hike north toward the Southwest Chute. Just east, at the bottom of Avalanche Glacier, you will see a rocky narrowing that makes the bottom of the Southwest Chute look like an hourglass. Hike up the 4,000-foot gully to False Summit in 3 to 4 hours.

The descent is straight down the chute, through the hourglass, to timberline. Again, use caution for avalanche danger if the snow is soft, and for falls if the snow is hard. If you are worried about conditions, descend the South Climb route (see Route 51). Once down to timberline, hike back to Cold Springs on the Round-the-Mountain Trail. Trees and snow cover at timberline may make the trail back to Cold Springs difficult to find. Be prepared to hike overland using a map and compass.

# Mount St. Helens

Mount St. Helens, at 8,365 feet, is one of the most well-known Cascade volcanos. Its May 18, 1980, eruption blew half the mountain away, including the top 1,321 feet. The Natives called the mountain "Loowit," and the Klickitat tribes translated this to "Fair Maiden" and the Salish to "Smoking One." On April 10, 1792, explorer Captain George Vancouver spied this peak from the Columbia River and named it after Britain's court ambassador to Madrid, Alleyne Fitzherbert, Baron St. Helens.

The first ascent was by *Oregonian* founder Thomas Dryer in 1853. The first ski descent was probably in 1961 by Fred Beckey, legendary Pacific Northwest mountaineer. The mountain was skied much from the north and south until the eruption in 1980 closed access for years. Since it reopened in 1987, climbing access is now exclusively from the south. The crater and the entire blown-out north side are closed to climbing.

The south side is accessed via two main sno-parks in the winter, Marble Mount and Cougar. In the summer, Climber's Bivouac parking area is the popular start. However, the road to Climber's Bivy doesn't open until May or June.

## Mount St. Helens Maps

USFS Gifford Pinchot National Forest, USFS Mount St. Helens National Volcanic Monument, Geo-Graphics Mount St. Helens National Volcanic Monument, Green Trails Mount St. Helens 364, Green Trails Mount St. Helens NW 364S

# Primary Info Centers/Ranger Districts

Mount St. Helens National Volcanic Monument: 360/247-3900; 24-hour recording at 360/247-3903, climbing recording at 360/247-3961, www.fs.fed.us/gpnf/mshnvm

# Avalanche/Weather/Road Conditions

Northwest Weather and Avalanche Center: 503/808-2400, www.nwac.noaa.gov

National Weather Service: 503/261-9246 or 360/694-6136, www.nws.noaa.gov

Washington DOT Pass Report: 888/766-4636, www.wsdot.wa.gov/sno-info

# Permits

A climbing permit is required year-round for making tracks above 4,800 feet. The system can be somewhat confusing. Also, things change. It's best to call well in advance to get the scoop. Following is the most recent update.

From November 1 to March 31, permits are free at a self-register station outside Jack's Restaurant in Cougar. Sounds easy, but it gets much more complicated.

From April 1 to May 14, the permits cost $15 a day but there is no limit to the number issued in a day. These are purchased from Jack's Restaurant, so call ahead to check on the hours it is open in spring, 360/231-4276.

From May 15 through October 31, $15 permits are limited to 100 a day, with 60 available for advance registration at the ranger station and at least 40 available the night before at Jack's Restaurant. At Jack's, the "night-before" permits are sold at 6:00 P.M. for the following day, but sign-up usually begins an hour earlier. If more than 40 people sign up before 6:00 P.M., a lottery determines the order in which permits are issued. One person can obtain permits for up to four people. Call ahead to confirm hours and to check how busy the previous week was.

Finally, you can buy a $30 Cascade Volcano Pass for Mount St. Helens and Mount Adams. However, you still need to acquire your climber's permit at Jack's as described above. The Volcano Pass is good for multiple climbs on both Mount St. Helens and Mount Adams.

A sno-park permit is required from October 1 to May 1 for Cougar and Marble Mount Sno-parks.

# 54 Monitor Ridge

❄❄❄❄❄

| | |
|---|---|
| Starting point | Climber's Bivouac, 3,800 feet |
| High point | Mount St. Helens Summit, 8,365 feet |
| Drive distance/time | 60 miles, 1.5 hours |
| Trail distance/time | 7 miles, 6 hours |
| Skill level | Advanced |
| Best season | Summer |
| Maps | USGS Mount St. Helens, Geo-Graphics Mount St. Helens National Volcanic Monument |

The Monitor Ridge route is a popular summer climb and a sweet glide. Like the South Climb on Mount Adams, this glisse descent is a great place to get mountaineering experience. The tour is a short, beautiful hike through the woods, a steady climb to the summit, and a fascinating look into the hissing, steaming crater: a Northwest classic.

Most people get their permits the night before, camp at Climber's Bivouac, and climb the next day round-trip to the summit.

Biffing it on St. Helens

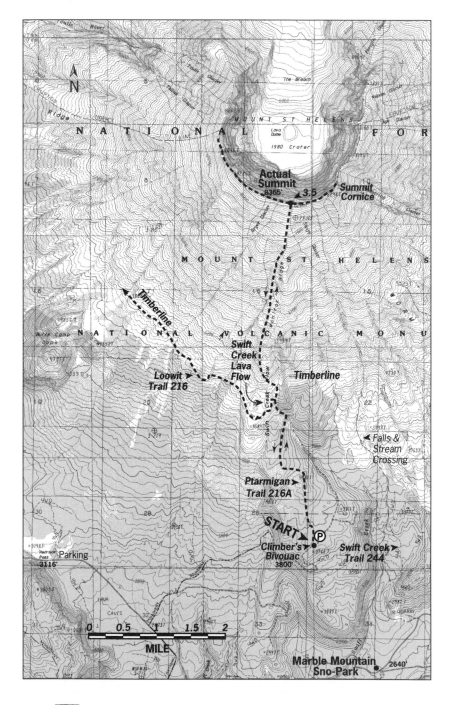

## Getting There

From Portland follow Interstate 5 north into Washington for 21 miles. Take exit 21 at Woodland and turn east on Washington 503. Drive toward Cougar about 20 miles. Just before town, obtain a permit at Jack's Restaurant on the south side of the road.

Continue east through Cougar as the road becomes Forest Road 90. About 4 miles past Cougar, the road turns north just past Swift Dam. A mile later, turn left on FR 83 and follow it for 3 miles. Turn left on FR 81. After a mile turn right onto gravel FR 830 to the Climber's Bivouac. The route is popular and marked by signs.

## The Route

From Climber's Bivouac follow Ptarmigan Trail 216A about 2 miles to timberline, where you pass Loowit Trail 216. Continue north on Trail 216A. When you break out of the trees, hike up a short slope to Monitor Ridge; the trail from here is marked by wood poles. The trail follows the ridge north directly to the summit rim, alternating on snow and a lava rock ridge, mostly on the rock until the final thousand feet. At the top, the true summit is a hundred feet west of Monitor Ridge. Use caution on the rim as the cornice overlooking the crater can avalanche.

The descent follows one of the main snowfields on Monitor Ridge. Descend the west or east side of the ridge following one of several snowfields. On the east-side drainage puts you right back at the Ptarmigan Trail. The west-side drainage requires more attention. When you are about 500 feet above timberline, hike back over Monitor Ridge and glide down the east side back to the Ptarmigan Trail. Use caution here: If you carve turns too far down one of the west-side drainages, you will end up west of the Ptarmigan Trail. If that happens, hike across the Swift Creek Lava Flow, also marked by poles, to get back to the Ptarmigan Trail.

# 55 Swift Creek

❄❄❄❄

| | |
|---|---|
| **Starting point** | Marble Mount Sno-park, 2,640 feet |
| **High point** | Mount St. Helens summit, 8,365 feet |
| **Drive distance/time** | 60 miles, 1.5 hours |
| **Trail distance/time** | 9 miles, 7 hours |
| **Skill level** | Advanced |
| **Best season** | Winter |
| **Maps** | USGS Mount St. Helens, Geo-Graphics Mount St. Helens National Volcanic Monument |

Swift Creek is the main winter route on the mountain. It is also known as Worm Flows, although the Worm Flows lava field is east of this route. Although it's not as popular as the summer route, lots of people will still be here, especially in May. Most people get up early and ski this in one day or camp just above timberline near the flats at the Swift Creek headwaters. You don't need to climb to the summit on this route: even an hour's hike above timberline yields sweet turns.

Camping at 7,000 feet, above Swift Creek headwaters, Mount St. Helens

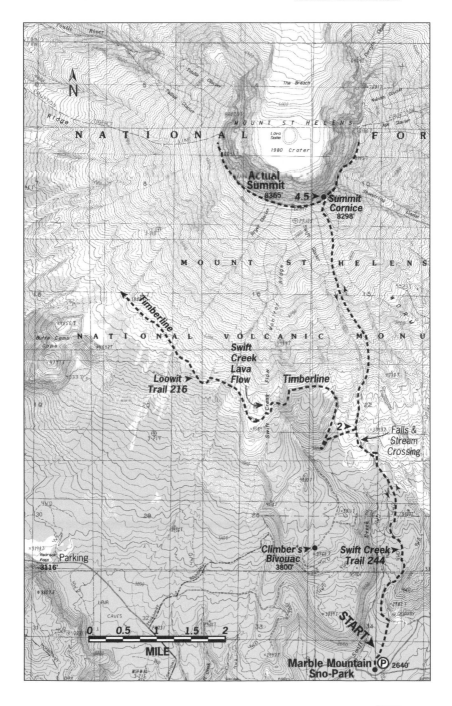

## Getting There

From Portland follow Interstate 5 north into Washington for 21 miles. Take exit 21 at Woodland and turn east on Washington 503. Drive toward Cougar about 20 miles. Just before town, obtain a permit at Jack's Restaurant on the south side of the road.

Continue east through Cougar as the road becomes Forest Road 90. About 4 miles past Cougar, the road turns north just past Swift Dam. A mile later, turn left on FR 83 and follow it east 5 miles to Marble Mount Sno-park. The route is popular and marked by signs.

## The Route

Head north on Swift Creek Trail 244 as it winds through the woods just to the east of Swift Creek. After 2 miles, the trail reaches timberline and crosses Loowit Trail 216. Continue north and cross over the Swift Creek headwaters just above a small waterfall. The unmarked trail heads across the wide, flat basin above the headwaters, where you will find several good campsites. From the flats, skin or snowshoe up the obvious main ridge toward the summit. This is a long snow climb, but you can stop and descend at any point.

Once on the crater rim, the true summit is a few hundred feet west, so you may choose to traverse. Use caution on the rim as the cornice overlooking the crater can avalanche.

The descent follows the main snowfield west or east of the climbing route. Steer clear of Monitor Ridge to the west, as frequent avalanches occur on the east-facing slope, and then slide close to the Swift Creek route.

Once back at the flats, make your way across the Swift Creek headwaters and find the Swift Creek Trail. With adequate snow cover, you should be able to ski or snowboard with poles back to the parking lot.

## 56 | MOUNT ST. HELENS
# Butte Dome
❄❄❄

| | |
|---|---|
| Starting point | Red Rock Pass, 3,116 feet |
| High point | Mount St. Helens summit, 8,365 feet |
| Drive distance/time | 60 miles, 1.5 hours |
| Trail distance/time | 10 miles, 8 hours |
| Skill level | Advanced |
| Best season | Spring |
| Maps | USGS Mount St. Helens, Geo-Graphics Mount St. Helens National Volcanic Monument |

This is a less popular route for skiing and snowboarding, mostly because the approach is significantly longer than the other routes. However, if you've done St. Helens by Monitor Ridge and Swift Creek and are looking for another challenge, this ascent will round out the south-side trio. In spring, you may have to park at Cougar Sno-park and skin up the road for 2 miles. Even if you can park at Red Rock Pass, this route is still longer than the other two.

Shredding the lava tube, Mount St. Helens

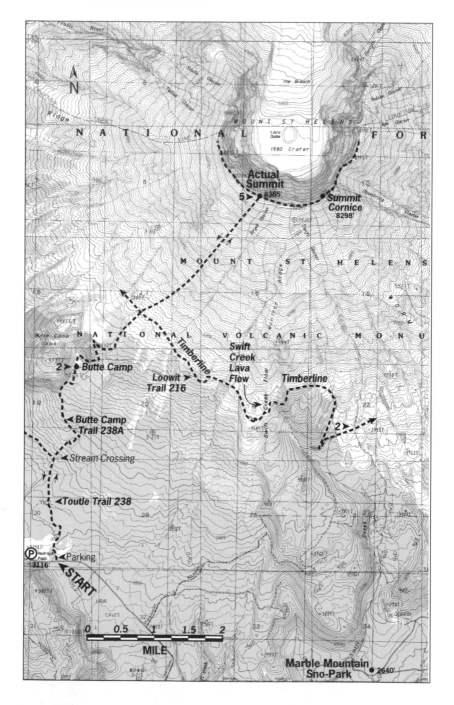

## Getting There

From Portland follow Interstate 5 north into Washington for 21 miles. Take exit 21 at Woodland and turn east on Washington 503. Drive toward Cougar about 20 miles. Just before town, obtain a permit at Jack's Restaurant on the south side of the road.

Continue east through Cougar as the road becomes Forest Road 90. About 4 miles past Cougar, the road turns north just past Swift Dam. A mile later, turn left on FR 83, go for 3 miles, then turn left on FR 81. If there is snow on the road, park at Cougar Sno-park at the junction of FR 83 and FR 81. In spring and summer, follow FR 81 about 2 miles to Red Rock Pass and the trailhead for the Toutle Trail.

## The Route

Head north on Toutle Trail 238 for a mile and continue on Butte Camp Trail 238A for 2 miles. Butte Camp is at 4,000 feet under Butte Dome, a small cinder cone. In another mile, the trail passes Loowit Trail 216 at timberline.

From timberline, follow the ridge to the summit. Because this route is unmarked, use caution in poor weather. Consider marking your trail and identify landmarks at timberline so you can find the trail home when you descend. The route puts you on the crater rim at the summit of St. Helens. Watch that you don't get too close to the edge, as the rim is a large cornice and can avalanche.

The descent follows the ascent route closely. Watch for landmarks to get back to the Butte Camp Trail. Veer too far in either direction and you may miss the trail home. Numerous gullies and drainages here eventually take you down to the Loowit Trail.

# Silver Star Mountain

Silver Star Mountain, 4,390 feet, is located in the far southwest corner of Gifford Pinchot National Forest and on land managed by the Washington Department of Natural Resources. Just above the cities of Vancouver and Camas, the snowcap can be seen from Portland and Interstate 84 while you're driving up the Columbia River Gorge. Although this is a popular summer destination, it is a rarely visited winter backcountry site.

With Silver Star's low elevation, the possibility of getting poor snow is significant. However, the drive from Portland is relatively short, and because Silver Star is visible from many parts of the metro area, this peak provides a constant reminder to get out and make turns.

## Silver Star Mountain Maps

USFS Gifford Pinchot National Forest, USFS Wind River Ranger District

## Primary Info Centers/Ranger Districts

Gifford Pinchot National Forest Headquarters, Vancouver, WA: 360/891-5000, 24-hour recording at 360/891-5009, www.fs.fed.us/gpnf

Wind River Ranger District: 509/427-3200

## Avalanche/Weather/Road Conditions

Northwest Weather and Avalanche Center: 503/808-2400, www.nwac.noaa.gov

National Weather Service: 503/261-9246 or 360/694-6136, www.nws.noaa.gov

Washington DOT Pass Report: 888/766-4636

## Permits

This area requires a Northwest Forest Pass year-round.

## SILVER STAR MOUNTAIN
# 57 Avrie's Glade
❄❄❄❄❄

| | |
|---|---|
| **Starting elevation** | Grouse Creek Vista, 2,400 feet |
| **High point** | Pyramid Rock, 3,200 feet |
| **Drive distance/time** | 40 miles, 1.5 hours |
| **Trail distance/time** | 2 miles, 3 hours |
| **Skill level** | Intermediate |
| **Best season** | Winter |
| **Maps** | USGS Larch Mountain, USGS Bobs Mountain |

Silver Star Mountain has several snow-covered slopes for backcountry turns. The most accessible is Avrie's Glade. This is a good route to have hiked previously in summer. In fact, some ancient Indian pits just below the summit make a great summer destination.

The roads are not plowed to the trailhead in winter. In big snow years, you may have a good month to ride Silver Star and a mile hike on slush to the trailhead. In light winters, the days that snow persists on the slopes may be few. Check with rangers regarding snow level; if the snow is melted on the road, it is likely too sparse to ride Avrie's Glade. Hint: Bring your rock skis or board.

Skinning to Pyramid Rock

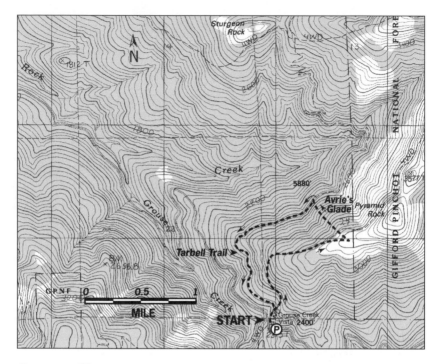

## Getting There

The trailhead at Grouse Creek Vista has two approaches: from the south via Washougal and from the west through Vancouver. The snow may melt faster on the south route and make it easier to follow. Take along road and Forest Service maps, and watch for signs to Grouse Vista Picnic Area when you are on gravel roads.

From Portland, head north over the Interstate 205 bridge into Washington. Just over the bridge, exit onto Washington 14 and head east toward Camas. At 10 miles, exit at Washougal on Washington 140/15th Street and at the "Washougal River Recreation Area" sign. Follow this road north out of town, then east as it winds along the Washougal River and becomes Washougal River Road. After 7 miles, turn left on Hughes Road toward Bear Prairie, which climbs through the woods for several miles. Turn onto Hughes Road and continue for 3 miles. Turn left on Skamania Mines Road/412th Avenue and follow it 3 miles to where it becomes DNR Road 1200 and heads to Grouse Creek Vista. Grouse Creek Vista is a wide spot in the road with room for parking at the saddle. If you drive too far, you will immediately start back down. The trailhead is marked on the north side.

# The Route

The Tarbell Trail and Trail 172 jointly leave the road and head north. After a few hundred yards, the trail forks and is marked by a sign. Head right on Trail 172 up a steep drainage toward Silver Star. The left fork is Tarbell Trail, on which you may return. Water may be draining on the trail and there may be downed trees and thick brush. After winding a few miles up a wooded drainage, Avrie's Glade opens up with Pyramid Rock in view and Silver Star Mountain beyond. Climb the knoll just to the south of Pyramid Rock for the best and closest line of descent.

Avrie's Glade is the broad, tree-covered slope below Pyramid Rock. The descent drops almost 1,000 feet until the trees and brush get too thick to ride through. At this point, you can skin or snowshoe back up for multiple runs. Stick to the trees for the safest route up. On your last run down, continue through the trees to the Tarbell Trail below the slope. The trail should be visible but snow-covered coming down from the large rock formation to the north called Sturgeon Rock. Once on the trail, hike a mile south back to Grouse Creek Vista.

# Mount Rainier

Mount Rainier, at 14,411 feet, is the tallest peak in the Pacific Northwest and the epicenter of Pacific Northwest mountaineering. It was called "Tahoma," or one of several variations of it, by Natives. British Captain George Vancouver spied the mountain in 1792 and named it for British naval officer Rear Admiral Peter Rainier. In 1899 it became the Unites States' fifth national park. The first ascent was made in 1870 by local mountaineers Hazard Stevens and Philemon Van Trump. The first ski ascent was done in 1939 by Sigurd Hall. Today, nearly 10,000 people attempt to climb to the summit yearly, and about half make it.

Numerous backcountry routes are found all around the mountain, especially on the south side. Skiing and snowboarding here are for experts, especially in winter or above timberline. Pacific storms pummel the mountain year-round. The weather can be horrendous, and ocean storms roll in quickly and with a vengeance. At Rainier, as at other volcanos in Oregon and Washington, cloud cap can settle on the peak for days at a time. You need excellent route finding and glacier travel skills at any time of year.

Although it requires a fairly long drive from Oregon, this mountain is a Pacific Northwest classic and a trip all Oregon ski and snowboard mountaineers make at one time or another. Detailed descriptions of the myriad descents are listed in *Backcountry Ski! Washington* by Seabury Blair, Jr. The Muir Snowfield, perhaps the most well-known spring/summer route, is just a sample.

## Mount Rainier Maps

NPS Mount Rainier National Park, Green Trails Mount Rainier East 270, Green Trails Mount Rainier West 269, Green Trails Paradise 270s

## Primary Info Centers/Ranger Districts

Mount Rainier National Park Headquarters: information at 360/569-2211, climber's recording at 360/569-2211, www.mount.rainier.national-park.com
Paradise Ranger Station: 360/569-2211, ext. 2328

# Avalanche/Weather/Road Conditions

Northwest Weather and Avalanche Center: 206/526-6677,
www.nwac.noaa.gov

National Weather Service: 503/261-9246 or 360/694-6136,
www.nws.noaa.gov

Washington DOT Pass Report: 888/766-4636, www.wsdot.wa.gov/sno-info

# Permits

A Mount Rainier National Park Permit ($10 for 7 days) or an annual
National Park permit is required to enter the park.

A climbing permit ($15 per person per climb or $25 per person for an
annual permit) is required to climb above 10,000 feet. Like the permits in the
fee demonstration program elsewhere, this permit covers safety, education,
human waste collection, and trail maintenance. Pre-climb registration is
required also, even for annual permit holders.

# 58 Muir Snowfield

❄❄❄❄❄

| | |
|---|---|
| Starting elevation | Paradise, 5,400 feet |
| High point | Camp Muir, 10,100 feet |
| Drive distance/time | 180 miles, 3 hours |
| Trail distance/time | 9 miles, 10 hours |
| Skill level | Advanced |
| Best season | Late spring, summer |
| Maps | USGS Mount Rainier East, USGS Mount Rainier West, Geo-Graphics Mount Rainier |

The Muir Snowfield is a classic, a must for all Pacific Northwest glisse alpinists. It was named for naturalist and mountaineer John Muir, after he climbed to this camp in 1883. It is the favorite route in summer for intermediate to advanced skiers and snowboarders. It is also on the way to Disappointment Cleaver, the easiest route to the summit, so it can be crowded with general mountaineers. If you catch this snowfield in late spring or early summer, shoot for a few days of clear weather and a high-pressure weather system. With any chance of foul weather rolling in from the Pacific, make alternate plans. It is a long drive just for rain.

## Getting There

Head north on Interstate 5 from Portland for about 70 miles to exit 68. Head east on U.S. 12 for 32 miles to Morton. Turn north on Washington 7 and drive 17 miles to Elbe. Turn east on Washington 706 and drive to the Nisqually entrance of the park. Obtain a park permit and continue about 20 miles to Paradise.

At Paradise, park in the overnight parking area. Sign in at the ranger station, obtain a climber's permit, and check conditions.

## The Route

From the Paradise parking lot, head north up the Skyline Trail to Alta Vista and Glacier Vista (6,300 feet). In winter this trail is well-traveled; in summer, the pavement shows. Continue to Panorama Point at 6,400 feet by following either the low-angle south-facing slope or the switchbacks on the west-facing slope. Both will be well-marked and well-traveled in summer.

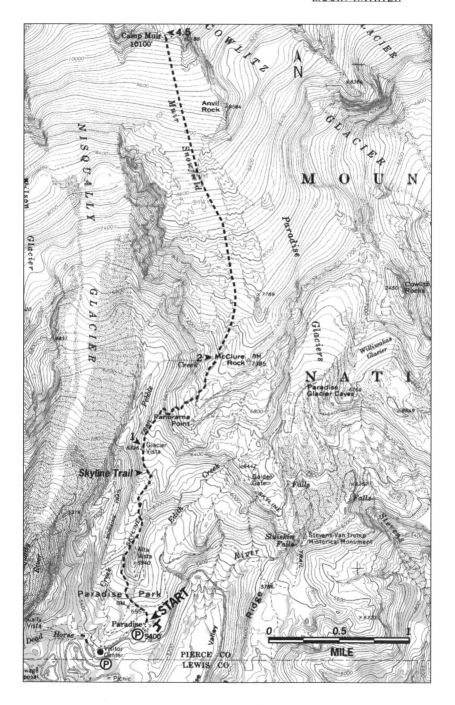

Continue north above Panorama Point to Pebble Creek, where you reach the terminus of the Muir Snowfield; McClure Rock will be to the east. It is a long trudge up the low-angle pitch to Camp Muir, resting at 10,100 feet, in a little notch below Disappointment Cleaver and the Nisqually Glacier. About halfway up you will see Anvil Rock off to the right.

The descent is a beautiful ride 4,000 feet down the Muir Snowfield, then down the steep sections below Panorama Point. It pretty much follows the route up. Depending on the snow coverage, you may have to hike out the last few miles.

Use extreme caution in foul weather or avalanche conditions. When descending below Camp Muir, one can accidentally head west and drop into the Nisqually Glacier, which is riddled with cliffs and crevasses. If you get too far to the east, you will drop into Paradise Glacier. Below Panorama Point the terrain is dangerous if avalanche conditions exist.

# Recommended Reading & Resources

## BOOKS

Barnett, Steve. *The Best Ski Touring in America*. San Francisco: Sierra Club, 1987.

Beckey, Fred. *Cascade Alpine Guide: Climbing and High Routes*. 3rd ed. Seattle: The Mountaineers, 1987.

Blair, Seabury Jr. *Backcountry Ski! Washington: The Best Trails and Descents for Free-heelers and Snowboarders*. Seattle: Sasquatch Books, 1998.

Burgdorfer, Rainier. *100 Classic Backcountry Ski and Snowboard Routes in Washington*. Seattle: The Mountaineers, 1999.

Carline, Jan D., Lentz, Martha J., and Macdonald, Steven C. *Mountaineering First Aid*. 4th ed. Seattle: The Mountaineers, 1996.

Daffern, Tony. *Avalanche Safety for Skiers & Climbers*. 2nd ed. Seattle: The Mountaineers, 1999.

Darvill, Fred. *Mountaineering Medicine and Backcountry Medical Guide*. 13th ed. Berkeley: Wilderness Press, 1998.

Dawson, Louis W. *Wild Snow: A Historical Guide to North American Ski Mountaineering*. Golden, CO: American Alpine Club, 1997.

Dodge, Nicholas A. *A Climber's Guide to Oregon*. Portland, OR: Mazamas, 1968.

Fredston, Jill A., and Fesler, Douglas S. *Snow Sense: A Guide to Evaluating Snow Avalanche Hazard*. Anchorage: Alaska Mountain Safety Center, 1999.

Graydon, Don, and Hanson, Kurt, eds. *Mountaineering: The Freedom of the Hills*. 6th ed. Seattle: The Mountaineers, 1997.

Humes, Jim, and Wagstaff, Sean. *Boarderlands: The Snowboarder's Guide to the West Coast*. San Francisco: HarperCollinsWest, 1995.

Kirkendall, Tom, and Spring, Vicky. *Cross-country Ski Tours: Washington's South Cascades and Olympics*. 2nd ed. Seattle: The Mountaineers, 1995.

Moynier, John. *Avalanche Aware: Safe Travel in Avalanche Terrain*. Helena, MT: Falcon Publishing, 1998.

Mueller, Ted. *Northwest Ski Trails*. Seattle: The Mountaineers, 1968.

Mueller, Ted, and Mueller, Marge. *Exploring Washington's Wild Areas: A Guide for Hikers, Backpackers, Climbers, Cross-country Skiers, and Paddlers*. Seattle: The Mountaineers, 1994.

O'Bannon, Allen, and Clelland, Mike, illus. *Allen and Mike's Really Cool Backcountry Ski Book: Traveling and Camping Skills for a Winter Environment*. Helena, MT: Falcon Publishing, 1996.

Powers, Phil. *NOLS Wilderness Mountaineering (NOLS Library)*. Mechanicsburg, PA: Stackpole Books, 2000.

Renner, Jeff. *Northwest Mountain Weather: Understanding and Forecasting for the Backcountry User.* Seattle: The Mountaineers, 1992.

Selters, Andy. *Glacier Travel & Crevasse Rescue.* Seattle: The Mountaineers, 1999.

Smoot, Jeff. *Summit Guide to the Cascade Volcanos.* Evergreen, CO: Chockstone, 1992.

Sullivan, William L. *100 Hikes in Southern Oregon.* Eugene, OR: Navillus Press, 1997

Sullivan, William L. *Exploring Oregon's Wild Areas: A Guide for Hikers, Backpackers, Climbers, Cross-country Skiers, and Paddlers.* 2nd ed. Seattle: The Mountaineers, 1994.

Thomas, Jeff. *Oregon High: A Climbing Guide.* Portland, OR: Keep Climbing Press, 1991.

Townsend, Chris. *Wilderness Skiing and Winter Camping.* Camden, ME: Ragged Mountain Press, 1994.

Van Tilburg, Christopher. *Backcountry Snowboarding.* Seattle: The Mountaineers, 1998.

Vielbig, Klindt. *Cross-Country Ski Routes Oregon: Includes Southwest Washington.* 2nd ed. Seattle: The Mountaineers, 1994.

Vielbig, Klindt. *Mount St. Helens National Volcanic Monument: A Complete Guide for Hiking, Climbing, Skiing, and Nature Viewing.* Seattle: The Mountaineers, 1997.

Vives, Jean. *Backcountry Skier.* Champaign, IL: Human Kinetics, 1998.

Waag, David L. *Oregon Descents: A Backcountry Ski Guide to the Southern Cascades.* Portland, OR: Free Heel Press, 1997.

## PERIODICALS

Coombs, Doug. "Hood: Commitment on the NE Face," *Couloir*, 1998, X(4), 18–21.

Craig, Stuart. "Studying the Classics," *Backcountry*, 1996, Mar:20–21.

Dappen, Andy. "20/20 Vision: The Wallowas Revisited," *Backcountry*, 1995, Oct, 10–15.

Dappen, Andy. "High on Hood," *Backcountry*, 1998, 14, 42–43.

Fawcett, Mark. "The Other Side of Mount Hood," *Snowboard Life*, 1997, 2(3), 106–112.

McGarr, Mike. "A Ski Descent of South Sister," *Mazama*, 1990:6.

Schechtel, Scott. "Icebergs in Oregon," *Backpacker*, 2000, 28(6):102–103.

Seidner, Read. "Adams: The Dark Horse," *Couloir*, 1998, 10(4), 42.

Seidner, Read. "Reality, Respect, Rainier," *Couloir*, 1998, 10(4), 40–41.

## WEB SITES *(accessed various times during 1998–2000)*

Bergfreunde Ski Club: www.bergfreunde.com

Cascade Mountaineers: users.bendnet.com/mountaineering/index.html

Chemetekans: www.chemeketans.org

Corvallis Mountain Rescue Unit: cmru.peak.org

Deschutes National Forest: www.fs.fed.us/r6/deschutes

Gifford Pinchot National Forest: www.fs.fed.us/gpnf

Hoodoo Ski Area: www.hoodoo.com

Mazamas: www.mazamas.org

Mount Bachelor Ski Area: www.mtbachelor.com

Mount Bailey Snowcats: www.mountbailey.com

Mount Hood Meadows Ski Area: www.skihood.com

Mount Hood National Forest: www.fs.fed.us/r6/mthood

Mount Hood Ski Patrol: www.skipatrol.mount-hood.or.us

Mount Rainier National Park: www.mount.rainier.national-park.com

Mount St. Helens National Volcanic Monument:
    www.fs.fed.us/gpnf/mshnvm

National Weather Service: www.nws.noaa.gov

Northwest Weather and Avalanche Center: www.nwac.noaa.gov

Oregon Department of Transportation: www.odot.state.or.us/roads

Oregon Mountaineering Association: www.i-world.net/oma

Oregon Nordic Club: www.onc.org

Oregon Ski and Snowboard Information: web.pdx.edu/~cyjh/orresorts.html

Pelican Butte: www.pelican2000.com

Portland Mountain Rescue: www.pmru.org

Ptarmigans: www.ptarmigans.org

Santiam Pass Ski Patrol: www.open.org/~spsp/intropg1.html

Ski Bowl Ski Area: www.skibowl.com

Summit Ski Area: www.summitskiarea.com

Timberline Ski Area: www.timberlinelodge.com

United States Forest Service Region 6: www.fs.fed.us/r6

Umpqua National Forest: www.fs.fed.us/r6/umpqua

Wallowa Alpine Huts: users.moscow.com/skihuts

## RECOMMENDED READING & RESOURCES

Wallowa–Whitman National Forest: www.fs.fed.us/r6/w–w

Washington Department of Transportation: www.wsdot.wa.gov/sno-info

Willamette National Forest: www.fs.fed.us/r6/willamette

Willamette Pass Ski Area: www.willamettepass.com

Winema National Forest: www.fs.fed.us/r6/winema

Wing Ridge Ski Tours: www.wingski.com

# Index

# Northwest Outdoors

## Backcountry Ski! Washington

The Best Trails & Descents for
Free-Heelers and Snowboarders

SEABURY BLAIR, JR.

*70 backcountry routes for all levels*

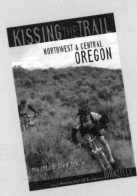

## Kissing the Trail: Northwest & Central Oregon

Mountain Bike Trails

JOHN ZILLY

*75 trails, all within 3 hours of Portland*

Also by John Zilly:
**Mountain Bike! Northwest Washington** (55 trails)
**Mountain Bike! Southwest Washington** (60 trails)

## Inside Out Oregon

A Best Places® Guide to the Outdoors

TERRY RICHARD

*The best of the state's year-round recreation —
plus Best Places® travel tips!*

Inside Out guides also available to:
• Washington • Northern California
• Southern California • British Columbia
• Northern Rockies

**SASQUATCH
BOOKS**

All Sasquatch recreation titles are available at bookstores and outdoors stores.
To order, call 1-800-775-0817 or visit www.SasquatchBooks.com.